D1117203

HENRY KISSINGER

Fred L. Israel

City College of New York

1986
CHELSEA HOUSE PUBLISHERS
NEW YORK
NEW HAVEN   PHILADELPHIA

SENIOR EDITOR: William P. Hansen
PROJECT EDITOR: John W. Selfridge
ASSOCIATE EDITOR: Marian W. Taylor
EDITORIAL COORDINATOR: Karyn Gullen Browne
EDITORIAL STAFF: Maria Behan
　　　　　　　Pierre Hauser
　　　　　　　Perry Scott King
　　　　　　　Kathleen McDermott
　　　　　　　Howard Ratner
　　　　　　　Alma Rodriguez-Sokol
　　　　　　　Bert Yaeger
ART DIRECTOR: Susan Lusk
LAYOUT: Irene Friedman
ART ASSISTANTS: Noreen Lamb
　　　　　　　Carol McDougall
　　　　　　　Victoria Tomaselli
COVER ILLUSTRATION: Kye Carbone
PICTURE RESEARCH: Karen Herman
　　　　　　　Matt Miller
　　　　　　　Elizabeth Terhune

Frontispiece courtesy of UPI/Bettmann Newsphotos

First Printing

Library of Congress Cataloging in Publication Data

Israel, Fred L. HENRY KISSINGER

(World leaders past & present)
Bibliography: p.
Includes index.
　　1. Kissinger, Henry, 1923–　　—Juvenile
literature.　2. Statesmen—United States—Biography—
Juvenile literature. [1. Kissinger, Henry, 1923–
2. Statesmen.　3. Nobel prizes—Biography]
I. Title.　II. Series.
E840.8.K58I84　　1986　　973.924'092'4　[B]　[92]　86-13712

ISBN 0-87754-588-X

Chelsea House Publishers

133 Christopher Street, New York, NY 10014

345 Whitney Avenue, New Haven, CT 06510

5014 West Chester Pike, Edgemont, PA 19028

Contents

ADENAUER
ALEXANDER THE GREAT
MARC ANTONY
KING ARTHUR
ATATÜRK
ATTLEE
BEGIN
BEN-GURION
BISMARCK
LÉON BLUM
BOLÍVAR
CESARE BORGIA
BRANDT
BREZHNEV
CAESAR
CALVIN
CASTRO
CATHERINE THE GREAT
CHARLEMAGNE
CHIANG KAI-SHEK
CHURCHILL
CLEMENCEAU
CLEOPATRA
CORTÉS
CROMWELL
DANTON
DE GAULLE
DE VALERA
DISRAELI
EISENHOWER
ELEANOR OF AQUITAINE
QUEEN ELIZABETH I
FERDINAND AND ISABELLA
FRANCO

FREDERICK THE GREAT
INDIRA GANDHI
MOHANDAS GANDHI
GARIBALDI
GENGHIS KHAN
GLADSTONE
GORBACHEV
HAMMARSKJÖLD
HENRY VIII
HENRY OF NAVARRE
HINDENBURG
HITLER
HO CHI MINH
HUSSEIN
IVAN THE TERRIBLE
ANDREW JACKSON
JEFFERSON
JOAN OF ARC
POPE JOHN XXIII
LYNDON JOHNSON
JUÁREZ
JOHN F. KENNEDY
KENYATTA
KHOMEINI
KHRUSHCHEV
MARTIN LUTHER KING, JR.
KISSINGER
LENIN
LINCOLN
LLOYD GEORGE
LOUIS XIV
LUTHER
JUDAS MACCABEUS
MAO ZEDONG

MARY, QUEEN OF SCOTS
GOLDA MEIR
METTERNICH
MUSSOLINI
NAPOLEON
NASSER
NEHRU
NERO
NICHOLAS II
NIXON
NKRUMAH
PERICLES
PERÓN
QADDAFI
ROBESPIERRE
ELEANOR ROOSEVELT
FRANKLIN D. ROOSEVELT
THEODORE ROOSEVELT
SADAT
STALIN
SUN YAT-SEN
TAMERLANE
THATCHER
TITO
TROTSKY
TRUDEAU
TRUMAN
VICTORIA
WASHINGTON
WEIZMANN
WOODROW WILSON
XERXES
ZHOU ENLAI

ON LEADERSHIP
Arthur M. Schlesinger, jr.

LEADERSHIP, it may be said, is really what makes the world go round. Love no doubt smooths the passage; but love is a private transaction between consenting adults. Leadership is a public transaction with history. The idea of leadership affirms the capacity of individuals to move, inspire, and mobilize masses of people so that they act together in pursuit of an end. Sometimes leadership serves good purposes, sometimes bad; but whether the end is benign or evil, great leaders are those men and women who leave their personal stamp on history.

Now, the very concept of leadership implies the proposition that individuals can make a difference. This proposition has never been universally accepted. From classical times to the present day, eminent thinkers have regarded individuals as no more than the agents and pawns of larger forces, whether the gods and goddesses of the ancient world or, in the modern era, race, class, nation, the dialectic, the will of the people, the spirit of the times, history itself. Against such forces, the individual dwindles into insignificance.

So contends the thesis of historical determinism. Tolstoy's great novel *War and Peace* offers a famous statement of the case. Why, Tolstoy asked, did millions of men in the Napoleonic wars, denying their human feelings and their common sense, move back and forth across Europe slaughtering their fellows? "The war," Tolstoy answered, "was bound to happen simply because it was bound to happen." All prior history predetermined it. As for leaders, they, Tolstoy said, "are but the labels that serve to give a name to an end and, like labels, they have the least possible connection with the event." The greater the leader, "the more conspicuous the inevitability and the predestination of every act he commits." The leader, said Tolstoy, is "the slave of history."

Determinism takes many forms. Marxism is the determinism of class. Nazism the determinism of race. But the idea of men and women as the slaves of history runs athwart the deepest human instincts. Rigid determinism abolishes the idea of human freedom—

the assumption of free choice that underlies every move we make, every word we speak, every thought we think. It abolishes the idea of human responsibility, since it is manifestly unfair to reward or punish people for actions that are by definition beyond their control. No one can live consistently by any deterministic creed. The Marxist states prove this themselves by their extreme susceptibility to the cult of leadership.

More than that, history refutes the idea that individuals make no difference. In December 1931 a British politician crossing Park Avenue in New York City between 76th and 77th Streets around 10:30 P.M. looked in the wrong direction and was knocked down by an automobile—a moment, he later recalled, of a man aghast, a world aglare: "I do not understand why I was not broken like an eggshell or squashed like a gooseberry." Fourteen months later an American politician, sitting in an open car in Miami, Florida, was fired on by an assassin; the man beside him was hit. Those who believe that individuals make no difference to history might well ponder whether the next two decades would have been the same had Mario Constasino's car killed Winston Churchill in 1931 and Giuseppe Zangara's bullet killed Franklin Roosevelt in 1933. Suppose, in addition, that Adolf Hitler had been killed in the street fighting during the Munich *Putsch* of 1923 and that Lenin had died of typhus during World War I. What would the 20th century be like now?

For better or for worse, individuals do make a difference. "The notion that a people can run itself and its affairs anonymously," wrote the philosopher William James, "is now well known to be the silliest of absurdities. Mankind does nothing save through initiatives on the part of inventors, great or small, and imitation by the rest of us—these are the sole factors in human progress. Individuals of genius show the way, and set the patterns, which common people then adopt and follow."

Leadership, James suggests, means leadership in thought as well as in action. In the long run, leaders in thought may well make the greater difference to the world. But, as Woodrow Wilson once said, "Those only are leaders of men, in the general eye, who lead in action. . . . It is at their hands that new thought gets its translation into the crude language of deeds." Leaders in thought often invent in solitude and obscurity, leaving to later generations the tasks of imitation. Leaders in action—the leaders portrayed in this series—have to be effective in their own time.

And they cannot be effective by themselves. They must act in response to the rhythms of their age. Their genius must be adapted, in a phrase of William James's, "to the receptivities of the moment." Leaders are useless without followers. "There goes the mob," said the French politician hearing a clamor in the streets. "I am their leader. I must follow them." Great leaders turn the inchoate emotions of the mob to purposes of their own. They seize on the opportunities of their time, the hopes, fears, frustrations, crises, potentialities. They succeed when events have prepared the way for them, when the community is awaiting to be aroused, when they can provide the clarifying and organizing ideas. Leadership ignites the circuit between the individual and the mass and thereby alters history.

It may alter history for better or for worse. Leaders have been responsible for the most extravagant follies and most monstrous crimes that have beset suffering humanity. They have also been vital in such gains as humanity has made in individual freedom, religious and racial tolerance, social justice and respect for human rights.

There is no sure way to tell in advance who is going to lead for good and who for evil. But a glance at the gallery of men and women in *World Leaders—Past and Present* suggests some useful tests.

One test is this: do leaders lead by force or by persuasion? By command or by consent? Through most of history leadership was exercised by the divine right of authority. The duty of followers was to defer and to obey. "Theirs not to reason why,/ Theirs but to do and die." On occasion, as with the so-called "enlightened despots" of the 18th century in Europe, absolutist leadership was animated by humane purposes. More often, absolutism nourished the passion for domination, land, gold and conquest and resulted in tyranny.

The great revolution of modern times has been the revolution of equality. The idea that all people should be equal in their legal condition has undermined the old structure of authority, hierarchy and deference. The revolution of equality has had two contrary effects on the nature of leadership. For equality, as Alexis de Tocqueville pointed out in his great study *Democracy in America,* might mean equality in servitude as well as equality in freedom.

"I know of only two methods of establishing equality in the political world," Tocqueville wrote. "Rights must be given to every citizen, or none at all to anyone . . . save one, who is the master of all." There was no middle ground "between the sovereignty of all and the absolute power of one man." In his astonishing prediction of 20th-century totalitarian dictatorship, Tocqueville explained how the revolution of equality could lead to the *"Führerprinzip"* and more terrible absolutism than the world had ever known.

But when rights are given to every citizen and the sovereignty of all is established, the problem of leadership takes a new form, becomes more exacting than ever before. It is easy to issue commands and enforce them by the rope and the stake, the concentration camp and the *gulag*. It is much harder to use argument and achievement to overcome opposition and win consent. The Founding Fathers of the United States understood the difficulty. They believed that history had given them the opportunity to decide, as Alexander Hamilton wrote in the first Federalist Paper, whether men are indeed capable of basing government on "reflection and choice, or whether they are forever destined to depend . . . on accident and force."

Government by reflection and choice called for a new style of leadership and a new quality of followership. It required leaders to be responsive to popular concerns, and it required followers to be active and informed participants in the process. Democracy does not eliminate emotion from politics; sometimes it fosters demagoguery; but it is confident that, as the greatest of democratic leaders put it, you cannot fool all of the people all of the time. It measures leadership by results and retires those who overreach or falter or fail.

It is true that in the long run despots are measured by results too. But they can postpone the day of judgment, sometimes indefinitely, and in the meantime they can do infinite harm. It is also true that democracy is no guarantee of virtue and intelligence in government, for the voice of the people is not necessarily the voice of God. But democracy, by assuring the right of opposition, offers built-in resistance to the evils inherent in absolutism. As the theologian Reinhold Niebuhr summed it up, "Man's capacity for justice makes democracy possible, but man's inclination to injustice makes democracy necessary."

A second test for leadership is the end for which power is sought. When leaders have as their goal the supremacy of a master race or the promotion of totalitarian revolution or the acquisition and exploitation of colonies or the protection of greed and privilege or the preservation of personal power, it is likely that their leadership will do little to advance the cause of humanity. When their goal is the abolition of slavery, the liberation of women, the enlargement of opportunity for the poor and powerless, the extension of equal rights to racial minorities, the defense of the freedoms of expression and opposition, it is likely that their leadership will increase the sum of human liberty and welfare.

Leaders have done great harm to the world. They have also conferred great benefits. You will find both sorts in this series. Even "good" leaders must be regarded with a certain wariness. Leaders are not demigods; they put on their trousers one leg after another just like ordinary mortals. No leader is infallible, and every leader needs to be reminded of this at regular intervals. Irreverence irritates leaders but is their salvation. Unquestioning submission corrupts leaders and demands followers. Making a cult of a leader is always a mistake. Fortunately hero worship generates its own antidote. "Every hero," said Emerson, "becomes a bore at last."

The signal benefit the great leaders confer is to embolden the rest of us to live according to our own best selves, to be active, insistent, and resolute in affirming our own sense of things. For great leaders attest to the reality of human freedom against the supposed inevitabilities of history. And they attest to the wisdom and power that may lie within the most unlikely of us, which is why Abraham Lincoln remains the supreme example of great leadership. A great leader, said Emerson, exhibits new possibilities to all humanity. "We feed on genius. . . . Great men exist that there may be greater men."

Great leaders, in short, justify themselves by emancipating and empowering their followers. So humanity struggles to master its destiny, remembering with Alexis de Tocqueville: "It is true that around every man a fatal circle is traced beyond which he cannot pass; but within the wide verge of that circle he is powerful and free; as it is with man, so with communities."

—*New York*

1

Honor and Despair

Shortly before 11 A.M. on the morning of October 16, 1973, an aide interrupted a White House meeting with an important dispatch. The message passed without comment to Secretary of State Henry Kissinger. Bulletin: Peace Prize. Oslo, Norway (AP) — U.S. Secretary of State Henry Kissinger and North Vietnamese Politburo member Le Duc Tho were awarded the 1973 Nobel Peace Prize today for their efforts to end the Vietnam War. Kissinger tossed the dispatch onto the table. His colleagues read it with astonishment rather than with jubilation. The Nobel Prize is presented annually in recognition of a single individual's contribution to the well-being of humanity. It is the highest award of its kind. Yet those present congratulated Kissinger without real passion. The official Nobel Committee of the Norwegian Parliament explained the award in terms of international relief at the end of the Vietnam War — "a wave of joy and hope to the entire world."

At age 50, Henry Kissinger became the 16th American to receive the coveted Nobel Peace Prize. He was the fifth secretary of state so honored, but the first to receive the award while in office.

Kissinger and Le Duc Tho, North Vietnamese Politburo member, in Paris, 1973. The two men were awarded the 1973 Nobel Peace Prize for their efforts to end the Vietnam War, but Le Duc Tho declined the prize and Kissinger sought to return his after the North Vietnamese captured Saigon in 1975.

The American ambassador to Norway, Thomas Ryan Byrne, accepted the Nobel Prize on behalf of Kissinger, who did not attend the ceremonies because of continued controversy over his direction of U.S. policy in Vietnam.

UPI/BETTMANN NEWSPHOTOS

Secretary of State Kissinger with U.S. President Richard M. Nixon in October 1973. Though Kissinger said during the 1968 campaign that Nixon was "the most dangerous, of all men running, to have as president," the two later found that they agreed on most issues of foreign policy and the uses of power.

The truce agreement between Kissinger and North Vietnamese leader Le Duc Tho had been reached on January 27, 1973, after months of tortuous negotiations and more than nine years of war. American combat forces then began a slow withdrawal from South Vietnam. While the truce had not brought peace to Southeast Asia, it marked the de-escalation of a terribly costly and unpopular war. Kissinger wrote, "In my bones I knew that collapse [of the agreement] was just a question of time. . . . The structure of peace was unlikely to last."

The awarding of a Nobel Peace Prize is usually a time of national pride for personal accomplishment. The award to Kissinger, however, further divided those who disagreed with American policy and actions in Vietnam. On December 10, 1973, the day of the presentation ceremony in Oslo, Kissinger used a pretext to be absent, and anti-American demonstrators tried to disrupt the proceedings. In an

The American evacuation of Saigon, April 1975. As the city fell to the North Vietnamese, Americans and their South Vietnamese dependents sought desperately to leave via U.S. Army airlifts. Here, an American uses force to deny a man entry to a crowded helicopter.

unprecedented sight, Norwegian King Olaf was jeered as he arrived to preside. The American ambassador, who read Kissinger's acceptance statement, cautiously entered the auditorium through a rear door to avoid confronting the hostile crowd. As Oslo's winter sun faded and the temperature dropped below freezing, some 5,000 people joined in a torchlight procession to the town center chanting obscenities against Kissinger and the United States. Posters, placards, leaflets, and handbills denounced the recipient. Rarely had the Norwegian capital witnessed such a great emotional demonstration.

Sixteen months later, on April 30, 1975, when the South Vietnamese capital of Saigon fell to the North Vietnamese, Kissinger returned the Nobel gold medal — "the peace we sought through negotiations has been overturned by force." The Nobel Committee insisted, however, that intervening events in no way diminished Kissinger's successful efforts to obtain a Vietnamese cease-fire agreement in 1973, and that he should keep the prize. At Kissinger's insistence, the cash portion of the prize, approximately $65,000, was donated to a scholarship fund for children of American servicemen killed or missing in action in Indochina.

> *What we have done is not a surrender. What we have done is give South Vietnam an opportunity to survive in conditions that are, today, political rather than military. It is now up to the South Vietnamese to win the political contest awaiting them.*
> —HENRY KISSINGER
> on the cease-fire agreement
> with North Vietnam

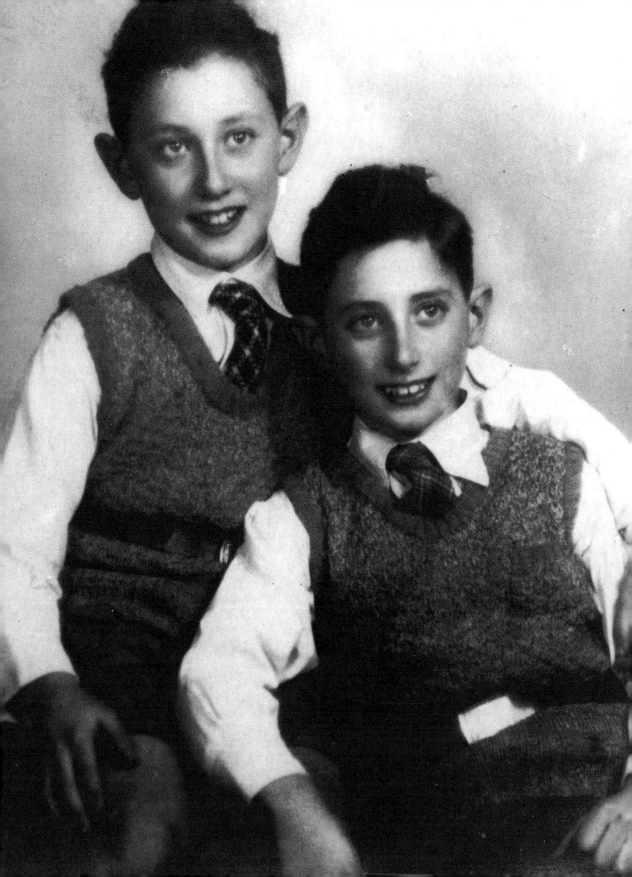

2

The Formative Years: Nazi Germany

One of America's glories is its tradition of opening its doors to political refugees and victims of war and persecution. Anti-Semitism in Germany forced Louis and Paula Kissinger, along with their two teenage sons, Henry and Walter, to flee the Nazis and to seek refuge in the United States in 1938.

Henry was born Heinz Alfred Kissinger on May 27, 1923, in the Bavarian city of Fürth, a few miles from Nuremberg. Henry Kissinger has been reluctant to discuss his early life in Germany. Commenting on his years in Fürth he wrote, "That part of my childhood is not a key to anything. . . . I was not consciously unhappy. I was not so acutely aware of what was going on. For children those things are not that serious. It is fashionable now to explain everything psychoanalytically, but let me tell you, the political persecutions of my childhood are not what control my life."

In his two-volume, 2,800-page memoir, Kissinger avoids mentioning his childhood; there is only a one-line mention of his parents, and no recollec-

UPI/BETTMANN NEWSPHOTOS

Louis and Paula Kissinger, Henry's parents, pictured in August, 1972. Paula told interviewers that the Kissinger children were subjected to beatings by Hitler Youth throughout their childhood.

Henry (left) and his brother Walter, ages 11 and 10, in 1933. Kissinger was born in the Bavarian city of Fürth, near Nuremberg, and grew up as Adolph Hitler and his Nazi party were gaining power.

UPI/BETTMANN NEWSPHOTOS

tions of Fürth or of his emigration to the United States as a teenager. Nevertheless, as Henry was growing up, the Nazis were gaining power throughout Germany, and it is likely that this historical time had a powerful effect on the young Kissinger.

Nazi storm troopers seized the city of Fürth in 1930, three years before the Nazi party took over the national government. Jews were forced to hide or flee for their own safety. "The extermination of all the Jews is not a necessary evil," shouted Hitler, "it is just necessary." Bands of roaming young people singing Hitler's praises torched the two local synagogues; Jewish-owned shops were forced to close; anti-Semitic slogans appeared on walls. "Our children weren't allowed to play with the others," Paula Kissinger told an interviewer in the 1970s.

Adolf Hitler. Kissinger has spoken very little of his youth under Hitler's murderous regime, saying that "the political persecutions of my childhood are not what control my life." Nonetheless, most observers feel he had to have been greatly influenced by such calamitous times.

A flag company of Hitler Youth parades in Nuremberg, 1938. The 1935 Nuremberg laws had revoked the German citizenship of Jews, forcing many to consider leaving the country.

"They stayed shut up in the garden. . . . The Hitler Youth, which included almost all the children in Fürth, sang in ranks in the street and paraded in uniform, and Henry and his brother would watch them, unable to understand why they didn't have the right to do what others did. . . . The two brothers stuck close together for protection."

In 1933 Louis Kissinger lost his teaching job at a secondary school for privileged girls because of a new regulation that prohibited Jews from holding government positions. He then took a much less prestigious post at a Jewish vocational school in Nuremberg, and hoped for the best. But, through terror and persecution, the Nazis had permanently disrupted Jewish lives — of Fürth's pre-1933 population of 3,000 Jews, only 70 were on hand to attend the first postwar religious service. In one of the few written references to his childhood, Kissinger noted that "though not practicing my religion, I could never forget that thirteen members of my family had died in Nazi concentration camps."

In 1935, Nuremberg laws revoked the German citizenship of Jews. Louis Kissinger lost his job at the vocational school, and his family was left with no income. They had lived in a spacious five-room apartment. Louis Kissinger, a deeply religious man, had raised his two sons accordingly. The household included many books on varied subjects as well as a number of musical instruments. Now it was time to leave. Jewish children could not attend public schools and when they ventured onto the playgrounds, Hitler Youth gangs beat them unmercifully. The soccer field where Henry played became a battleground. By 1938 Jews of Fürth were being murdered in the streets, "It was my wife who got us out of Germany," Louis Kissinger said of their escape. "Paula had an aunt in London. We took the boys there, and then after a few weeks came to America. . . . We have been back to Germany only twice since . . . to visit the graves of our parents. Otherwise — well, you can understand, I am sure, how we felt." In later years, however, Henry Kissinger commented: "My life in Fürth passed without leaving any lasting impressions." One incident he did recall: "The other children beat us up."

The Kissinger family settled in the then predominantly Jewish Washington Heights section of New York City. Louis, age 50, found work as a bookkeeper and his wife cooked Jewish delicacies for well-to-do neighbors. Henry learned English and entered Manhattan's George Washington High School in September 1938, graduating in 1941 with a straight "A" average. He switched to night school so that he could contribute to the family income by working in a shaving brush factory by day. "I always remembered the thrill when I first walked the streets of New York City," recalled Kissinger. "Seeing a

As an historian, you have to be conscious of the fact that every civilization that has ever existed has ultimately collapsed.

—HENRY KISSINGER
quoted from an interview
with *The New York Times,*
October 13, 1974

group of boys, I began to cross to the other side to avoid being beaten up. And then I remembered where I was."

In June 1941 Kissinger enrolled in the summer night school program at the City College of New York, in hopes of becoming an accountant. "For a refugee," he recalled, "it was the easiest profession to get into." In January 1942 he transferred to City College's School of Business Administration.

During these years, Kissinger was exposed to

> *From his two experiences in Nazi Germany, Kissinger later drew many lessons. He came to feel deeply the 'tragic' sense of life, the way in which what was ascendant in history could be brought low; this was a sense he felt totally lacking in the American people, and which he felt he as a 'European' could supply. He turned against revolutionary movements, which could dispossess people of their lifelong status and humiliate them. . . . And last, he became convinced that 'goodwill' was not enough.*
> —BRUCE MAZLISH
> American historian

Jewish man in Nazi Germany, 1941, wearing the compulsory yellow star. Under Hitler's campaign to rid the country of Jews and other "undesirables," the Jewish population of Fürth was decimated — from 3,000 before 1933 to just 70 after the war, a pattern that was duplicated throughout Europe.

German refugees arriving in New York City, 1938. That year the Kissingers, like many other Jewish families, fled Germany, following a long period of persecution, and settled in America.

American ways of life, attending Yankee baseball games and taking summer trips to the Catskills (a popular resort area in upstate New York). But the process of Americanization was never totally completed; Kissinger's taste and style would always be distinctly European, with a deep and enduring affinity for European ways. He learned quickly, but always spoke with a decidedly German accent. "I was terribly self-conscious about it," he would say years later.

One evening in January 1943, Kissinger came home from his night course to find an official-looking letter. It was a draft notice. At age 19, he was inducted into the United States Army. (On June 19, 1943, Kissinger became a naturalized American citizen.)

Kissinger saw 16 weeks of rugged basic training in North Carolina. A superior grade on an IQ test placed Kissinger in the Army Special Training Program (ASTP) at Lafayette College in Easton, Pennsylvania. (An associate in the program described

Kissinger as "the brainiest of a very intelligent class.")

After the program, Kissinger joined the Eighty-fourth Infantry Division at Camp Claiborn, Louisiana. In 1944 Private Kissinger reversed his itinerary of six years earlier. He returned to Germany, but this time with a combat unit fighting the Nazis. Because of his knowledge of German, the division's general made Kissinger his driver-interpreter.

In 1945, 21-year-old Kissinger was given the assignment of re-establishing a working government in the German city of Krefeld in the North Rhine-

Concentration camp inmates upon their liberation in April 1945. In one of his few comments about his childhood, Kissinger wrote, "I could never forget that 13 members of my family had died in the concentration camps."

AP/WIDE WORLD

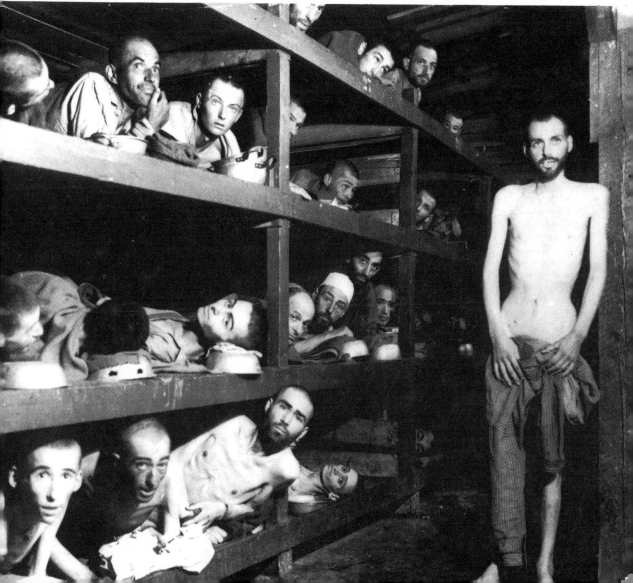

German children foraging for food, November 1945. World War II left Germany devastated, looking like "one vast rubble dump," as some historians have said, and requiring the help of American, Soviet, French, and British occupying forces to rebuild the postwar German economy.

Westphalia state. Though the city had been left in ruins by retreating Nazis, within a week Kissinger's infantry division got the municipal government back on its feet. The achievement at Krefeld was repeated in the district of Bergstrasse in Hesse, 100 miles west of Fürth.

Contemporaries noted that although Kissinger had the authority of a military governor with broad powers, including that of arrest without questions, he showed total impartiality and superb administrative skills. His German secretary at the time recalls him saying repeatedly, "We have not come here for revenge," and she added, "You know in those days right after the war, this sort of attitude was far from taken for granted." In 1946, having earned the rank of sergeant and a Bronze Star for outstanding military service, Kissinger was discharged. However, because of his superior intellectual ability, the Army kept him on in Germany as a civilian instructor at the European Command Intelligence School at Oberammergau, where he trained American intelligence agents in German history.

The horror of Nazi Germany seems to have influenced Kissinger's later writings and thought in that they display a great fear of social chaos, internal political upheaval, and international instability.

U.S. troops walking through the ruins of Krefeld, Germany, in 1945. Kissinger, who served in Germany during the war as a U.S. Army interpreter, stayed on afterward as a military governor and garnered wide praise for his efforts at rebuilding Krefeld and other German areas.

3

The Making of a Leader

In the fall of 1947 Kissinger entered Harvard University on a scholarship. He majored in philosophy, and graduated with a Bachelor of Arts degree in 1950. His 350-page undergraduate thesis, which he called *The Meaning of History*, resulted in Harvard setting a 150-page limit on all future undergraduate theses. The new ruling would have made little difference for Kissinger because his mentor read but the first 100 pages and deemed it a work of the highest distinction. In a word, Kissinger's undergraduate record was brilliant; he graduated Phi Beta Kappa and *summa cum laude*.

In his final undergraduate year, Kissinger married Anneliese Fleischer. Socially and financially a cut above the Kissingers, the Fleischers had been successful shoe merchants in Bavaria before fleeing the Nazis in 1937. "Ann" was not an intellectual and had no interest in academics or foreign affairs. Still, she and Kissinger maintained a close relationship during his years of military service and, later, while he was a young, struggling academic. The newlyweds moved into a Boston apartment, and Kissinger began his graduate work.

Kissinger in 1959. Through his work at Harvard University, Kissinger had by this time become a celebrity, in both academic and government circles, for his insightful writings on the nation's defense and nuclear policies.

UPI/BETTMANN NEWSPHOTOS

Dr. William Yandell Elliott, a professor in Harvard's government department. Kissinger became a disciple of Elliott, who appointed him executive director of the university's International Seminar, through which Kissinger was exposed for the first time to leading politicians and intellectuals from around the world.

Funded by scholarships, Kissinger completed his Ph.D. in 1956. In those days, Harvard exempted *summa cum laude* students from doctoral oral exams. This set Kissinger apart from other graduate students both in his own perception of himself and in the way his fellow graduate students perceived him. Rather than studying for his orals, Kissinger assisted professors with their research, writing, and administrative responsibilities.

In those hectic postwar days, Harvard expanded with a frenzy. A year hardly passed without the opening of some new institute or special program, and Kissinger took on all types of responsibilities assigned by his professors. Often arrogant and always argumentative, Kissinger was described by an old friend as the sort of person who knows he is bright but assumes others will not recognize it unless he tells them. Kissinger's doctoral dissertation, *A World Restored: Metternich, Castlereagh, and the Restoration of Peace, 1812*, won the Sumner Prize for distinguished scholarly achievement and was published in 1957.

A World Restored praised the "conference system," which resolved the chaos caused by the Napoleonic wars and which launched Europe on a century of relative stability before the cataclysmic outbreak of World War I in 1914. The conference system had been built not by kings or armies but by a few clever foreign ministers who monopolized the diplomatic process. Through their political and intellectual abilities, grand diplomacy, and military strength these ministers preserved European order and stability for almost 100 years. "It may not have fulfilled all the hopes of an idealistic generation," wrote Kissinger, "but it gave this generation something perhaps more precious: a period of stability which permitted their hopes to be realized without a major war or a permanent revolution." Perhaps emerging in Kissinger's mind was a grand plan for modern international relations based on nineteenth-century balances of power. As he wrote in 1969, "We believe that the paramount problem of our time is the achievement of a stable peace in which different systems coexist with each other."

> *Instinct is not a guide to political conduct. Effective leadership is always forced — whatever its motives — to represent itself as the carrier of ideas embodying purposes. All truly great achievements in history resulted from the actualization of principles, not from the clever evaluation of political conditions.*
> —HENRY KISSINGER
> in his undergraduate thesis,
> *The Meaning of History*

At Harvard, Kissinger became the disciple of a professor of government named William Yandell Elliott, who involved him in a unique program, the Harvard International Seminar. Funded by the Ford Foundation and the Rockefellers' Asia Foundation, the seminar brought to Harvard persons between the ages of 26 and 45 who were on the verge of reaching leadership positions in their respective countries, so they could learn about America from various perspectives. In 1951 Professor Elliott had Kissinger, now 28, whom he described "more like a mature colleague than a student," named executive director of the program.

Between 1952 and 1969, more than 600 "future leaders" from Western Europe, Asia, Latin America, and Africa participated in the program. Kissinger selected the seminar members, arranged to bring them to the United States, and guided the six-week program each summer. Participants included Ja-

Engraving depicting the Congress of Vienna, 1814–15. That gathering of European leaders following the fall of Napoleon ushered in a century of relative peace and was the basis for Kissinger's doctoral dissertation, *A World Restored*.

Atomic bomb test in the Bikini Islands, 1950. Kissinger's famous 1957 report, *Nuclear Weapons and Foreign Policy*, **criticized America's nuclear weapons policy, became a nationwide bestseller, and brought him to the attention of President Dwight D. Eisenhower, for whom he soon became an adviser.**

pan's future prime minister Nakasone; future president of France Giscard; future Israeli foreign minister Allon; future Belgian prime minister Tindemans; future Norwegian foreign minister Frydenlund; and future leader of Great Britain's Labour party Foot. Above all, the seminar gave Kissinger an extraordinary access to foreign intellectuals and future policy makers. With money from a Rockefeller Brothers Fund grant, Kissinger, with Elliott's help, established *Confluence* in 1952, a scholarly journal in which some of the world's most renowned political experts debated international policy issues.

In 1955 Harvard denied Kissinger a tenured teaching position. He did, however, get a "big break" that year. The managing editor's position at the prestigious journal *Foreign Affairs* became vacant. Hamilton Fish Armstrong, the editor, asked friends at Harvard to recommend candidates. Arthur Schlesinger, jr., then professor of history at Harvard, suggested Kissinger. After an interview, Armstrong thought Kissinger's writing and analytical skills could better be used in another capacity.

The Council on Foreign Relations, which publishes *Foreign Affairs*, had been conducting a study of nuclear weapons and their effect on foreign policy. There are many councils at Harvard but the extremely influential Council on Foreign Relations articulates the intellectual basis for American foreign policy. From its membership come policy planners and decision makers—their overriding concern is the need for a safe international order carefully sculpted by American power. Armstrong suggested Kissinger coordinate the 34-man panel and write the final report. The council agreed after receiving outstanding letters of recommendation from Elliott, Schlesinger, and McGeorge Bundy, then dean of the Harvard faculty.

The result was Kissinger's *Nuclear Weapons and Foreign Policy*, published in 1957 under the council's auspices. The book, which remained on the best-seller list for 14 weeks, was read by then Vice-President Richard Nixon, who sent Kissinger a congratulatory note. The central argument of the work is a criticism of defense planners for not considering an alternative to full-scale nuclear war. The book suggests another approach in which nuclear weapons could be used in a limited war while the United States made its goals known through diplomacy, avoiding an all-out nuclear conflagration. "Force by itself will not supply an answer to the challenge of the future. . . . In Greek mythology, Nemesis, the goddess of fate, sometimes punished man by fulfilling his wishes too completely. It has remained

Although accepted by the admissions department as an undergraduate, it was clear to someone of [Kissinger's] sensitivity that he was not part of the 'real' Harvard: the Harvard of clubs, sports and weekend parties. He was always on the periphery, a tolerated guest in the drafty halls outside the warm banquet room.
—BRUCE MAZLISH
American historian

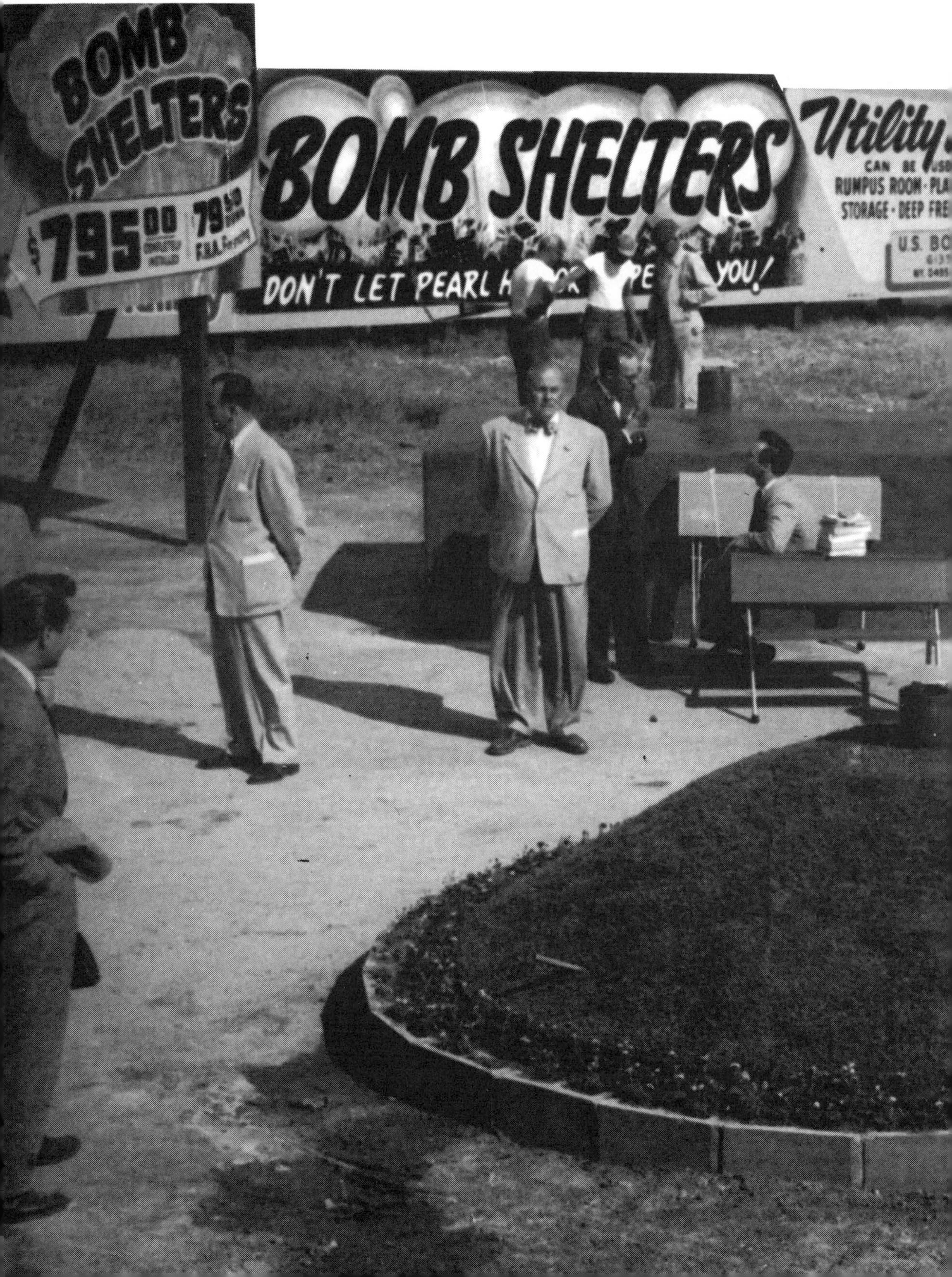
BOMB SHELTERS
$795.00
BOMB SHELTERS

Billboard advertising bomb shelters, Los Angeles, 1951. Kissinger's report argued that nuclear weapons could be used in a "limited" exchange, rather than the "massive retaliation" that was the standard idea of U.S. defense strategists. The idea intrigued some people but scared many others.

for the nuclear age to experience the full irony of this penalty."

A few pages later, Kissinger cites the Prometheus legend: "Our generation has succeeded in stealing the fire of the gods and it is doomed to live with the horror of its achievement." Of pre-1914 Europe, he writes, "In the long interval of peace the sense of the tragic was lost; it was forgotten that states could die, that upheavals could be irretrievable." He goes on to say, "Nothing is more difficult for Americans to understand than the possibility of tragedy."

Kissinger's thesis that a nuclear war could be limited clashed with the ideas of Washington strategists who believed that any nuclear war would become a total conflagration. Kissinger, at the age of 34, became a celebrity both in academic and policy-making circles. His book established him internationally as one of the foremost "defense intellectuals" in the United States and placed him increasingly in demand as an adviser to the highest levels of government. He had moved to the forefront of that small segment of the academic community that dealt with nuclear and national strategy, the

Nelson Rockefeller and Dwight D. Eisenhower, December 1954. Rockefeller was then serving as the president's special assistant for national security. He and Kissinger would soon form a close friendship that would help both men's political aspirations.

UPI/BETTMANN NEWSPHOTOS

Dr. Henry Kissinger

Kissinger in 1957. At the time, Kissinger's continued prominence at Harvard, coupled with an increasingly influential role as a defense consultant to the Eisenhower administration, made him a charismatic yet controversial figure.

scholarly technocrats of current affairs.

Kissinger's work for the Council on Foreign Relations brought him to New York, where he gained the attention of David Rockefeller, a member of the study group on nuclear weapons. Previously, in late 1955, Kissinger had met Nelson Rockefeller, at that time President Dwight D. Eisenhower's special assistant for national security affairs. The Rockefeller Brothers Fund had begun a special study of major international problems that the United States would be facing in the near future. Nelson had asked a group of prominent Americans, among whom Kissinger was included, to articulate the nation's long-range objectives. Kissinger became the director of this highly influential group. The project lasted 28 months and the final report was published on the front page of *The New York Times*, January 7, 1958.

Of greater importance for Kissinger was that he became a trusted friend and adviser to Nelson Rockefeller, who had presidential aspirations.

Nelson Rockefeller and Henry Kissinger, though on the surface an unlikely pair, formed a perfect professional relationship. Nelson became the passionate seeker of political office who immersed himself in campaign strategies, while Kissinger, a political expert, provided sound advice. Rockefeller had Kissinger's complete trust and loyalty. They each sincerely believed in the greatness of the United States and its role as the major force of stability in every area of the world. Kissinger eventually described Nelson Rockefeller as "the single most influential person in my life," and it is to him that Kissinger dedicated the first volume of his memoirs.

Kissinger returned to Harvard in the fall of 1957 as assistant director of the Center for International Affairs and director of Harvard's Defense Studies program with a simultaneous appointment in the government department. He rapidly rose through the academic ranks to full professor in 1962, and his association with the Council on Foreign Relations had given him celebrity status.

In Harvard's fiercely competitive environment, Kissinger caused no small resentment among those colleagues who felt slighted by his privileged status. His students, however, generally rated him as a stimulating and superior instructor deeply interested in the subject matter. They said his lectures vibrated with an excitement derived from the urgency of his thoughts. Kissinger could radiate

President John F. Kennedy, center, conducting a meeting during the Cuban Missile Crisis in October 1962. Kissinger had earlier left his post as Kennedy's special assistant for national security affairs after failing, in his own view, to adjust to the confrontational style of the Kennedy administration.

enormous charm. His authoritative command of language, combined with his soft-spoken manner and his wry, often self-deprecating wit, made him a most popular lecturer.

Concurrently with his Harvard duties, 1955–60, Kissinger served as a consultant to the Eisenhower administration in the area of weapon systems analysis. With John F. Kennedy's 1960 presidential victory, many Harvard academics went to Washington as members of the new administration. Arthur Schlesinger, jr. and McGeorge Bundy introduced Kissinger to President Kennedy.

Bundy, who left his Harvard position to become Kennedy's special assistant on national security, invited Kissinger to serve as a White House consultant on military and security policy. This appointment, though rarely placing him at the center of activity, afforded Kissinger, now 38, frequent opportunities to confer with Western European leaders.

Meanwhile Kissinger's family life was taking new turns. He and his wife had bought a house two years prior to his appointment as White House consultant, and had begun planning to have a family. In 1960 their first child, Elizabeth, was born; in 1962 they had a son, David. But the marriage began to falter, and within a year after the birth of their second child, the couple separated. A year later, they were divorced.

Kissinger experienced a lull in his career during the trials of his failing marriage. To some White House officials, Kissinger became a nuisance. An aide to Bundy recalled: "After the first year I think Henry became a needler and a critic, and when you're under the kind of pressure you are in Washington, you tend not to want to bring people from a distance to needle you and criticize you." Above all, it seems that both politically and stylistically, Kissinger did not seem too well suited for the Kennedy White House. "It was less Henry's views than his style which hurt him," recalls a colleague.

Perhaps at this point, Kissinger realized that any future access to power must come from his inner motivation and personality — not from his raw intellectual energy. "With little understanding then of

We met every week for years. Elliott made me discover Dostoevski, Hegel, Kant, Spinoza and Homer. On many Sundays we took long walks in Concord. He spoke of the power of love, and said that the only truly unforgivable sin is to use people as if they were objects. He discussed greatness and excellence. And while I did not always follow his words I knew I was in the presence of a remarkable man.
—HENRY KISSINGER
describing his relationship
with his mentor,
Harvard professor
William Yandell Elliott

Kissinger appears at a New York hotel in 1973 to attend a dinner honoring his efforts to achieve international peace. With him are his father and his son, David.

how the presidency worked, I consumed my energies in offering unwanted advice and, in our infrequent contact, inflicting on President Kennedy learned disquisitions about which he could have done nothing even in the unlikely event that they aroused his interest. It was with a sense of mutual relief that we parted company in mid-1962."

"One of the things he learned," states another associate in discussing Kissinger's experience with the Kennedy White House, "is that the only way to deal effectively with people at that level is to wait for them to call you and tell you that they want to hear

Nelson Rockefeller campaigning in New York City, June 1968. Kissinger, Rockefeller's principal adviser on foreign affairs, later wrote that he was "the single most influential person in my life" for his belief in American values and in the need for a major U.S. role overseas.

what you have to say."

During the 1960s Kissinger became well known for his close, ongoing association with then governor of New York, Nelson Rockefeller. As one of Rockefeller's advisers, Kissinger gave his total effort to the governor's 1968 bid for the Republican presidential nomination. He put in long days — speaking with Rockefeller in New York about foreign policy issues in the morning and meeting his classes at Harvard in the afternoon. When asked to clarify Rockefeller's foreign policy views, the governor's aides would tell reporters: "Go see Henry. He's the only one around here who can explain what our position is and make it come out sounding right."

Through three Republican conventions (1960,

1964, and 1968), Rockefeller fought for his ideas and values, especially regarding foreign policy, only to lose out to the more conservative wing of the Republican party. Rockefeller intensely disliked his 1968 opponent, Richard Nixon. Besides personal differences, Rockefeller sincerely believed Nixon to be the worst kind of political opportunist who lacked the vision and idealism needed to shape America's destiny.

Nixon had served as vice-president under President Eisenhower from 1953 to 1961 and would be elected president of the United States in 1968, defeating Senator Hubert Humphrey. To some, Nixon seemed power-mad, unscrupulous, and so vehemently anti-communist that he could very well lead the United States into a nuclear war with the Soviet Union. Just prior to the 1968 Republican convention, Kissinger was quoted as saying: "Richard Nixon is the most dangerous, of all men running, to have as president."

On the other hand, Rockefeller, Kissinger's patron, could do no wrong — "Of all the public figures I have known, he retained the most absolute, almost touching, faith in the power of ideas. He spent enormous resources to try to learn what was 'the right thing' to do. His national campaigns were based on the illusion that the way to win delegates at national political conventions was to present substantive programs. . . . Nelson Rockefeller, I am certain, would have made a great president."

Nixon, the consummate politician, crushed Rockefeller and won the Republican nomination on the first ballot. Kissinger often referred disparagingly to "that man Nixon," who, he said, "doesn't have the right to rule."

In his acceptance speech, Nixon welcomed the support of the "silent majority" of "forgotten Americans" — "the non-shouters, the non-demonstrators." Nixon's victory, however, was bittersweet in that he obtained a mere 43.4% of the popular vote, the lowest for a successful candidate since Woodrow Wilson in 1912.

Kissinger and Rockefeller were both shocked when Richard Nixon asked Kissinger to become his

When Nelson buys a Picasso, he does not hire four housepainters to improve it.
—HENRY KISSINGER after a speech he wrote for Nelson Rockefeller was rewritten by four of the New York governor's aides

assistant for national security, one of the most important foreign policy positions in a presidential administration. Nixon was choosing as a chief adviser a man he barely knew and who had been associated intimately with his political enemies. If Kissinger had been anti-Nixon, Nixon certainly was not anti-Kissinger.

Nixon's choice of Kissinger still remains an enigma. Why Kissinger? Perhaps he was chosen to show both Republican and Democratic liberals that they had erred in describing Nixon as a saber rattling, cold war warrior — after all, his principal foreign policy adviser would be a college professor lured away from Harvard. Perhaps Nixon realized that he needed someone to articulate a coherent conceptual framework for his many foreign policy statements and that Kissinger shared his pragmatic, rather than idealistic perception of the world. Starting from totally different backgrounds, the grocer's son from Whittier, California, and the refugee from Hitler's Germany seemed to have reached similar positions on policy and the uses of power. William Safire, then a Nixon speechwriter, noted that the president-elect took a certain delight in offering "one of the crown jewels in the Rockefeller diadem," a position Kissinger could not refuse.

For years, Kissinger had been shuttling between Harvard and Washington offering his opinions as a consultant, always on the outskirts of political influence. When asked to move into center stage, Kissinger found this offer irresistible, stating "if I rejected the offer I would blame myself for every future failure of foreign policy." (Ironically, Hubert Humphrey revealed years later that if he had won the 1968 election he, too, would have asked Kissinger to serve as his foreign policy adviser.) Nelson Rockefeller agreed, telling him such a request was a duty and that to refuse would be an act of pure selfishness.

In fact, praise for Kissinger's appointment came from both liberals and conservatives. "Not since Florence Nightingale," quipped conservative columnist William F. Buckley, "has any public figure received such public acclamation." A study of Henry

Rockefeller is the only candidate at this time who could unite the country, who could appeal to Democrats and Independents with a program that could look to the future and focus America on its purposes.
—HENRY KISSINGER
in a radio interview during
the 1968 Republican
National Convention

Kissinger from this point in his life is necessarily a study of American foreign policy, its achievements and disappointments.

On January 20, 1969, Richard Nixon took the presidential oath, swearing, as did his 36 predecessors, to "preserve, protect, and defend the Constitution of the United States." Kissinger wrote, "My own feeling of surprise at being there was palpable. Only eight weeks earlier the suggestion that I might participate in the inauguration as one of the new president's closest advisers would have seemed preposterous." And so Henry Kissinger, national security adviser at the age of 46, had the awesome responsibility of advising the president of the United States on the solemn responsibilities described in the presidential oath.

In addition to being the president's personal assistant on all foreign relations matters, Kissinger

Richard Nixon and his supporters at the Republican party convention in 1968. When Nixon crushed Rockefeller to secure the GOP nomination on the first ballot — a victory that also signaled a rejection of Kissinger's views on the Vietnam War — Kissinger claimed that Nixon "doesn't have the right to rule."

Nixon and Kissinger after the announcement of Kissinger's appointment as the president's special assistant for national security affairs in December 1968. Kissinger's apparent about-face in his regard for the president-elect was denounced by many as opportunistic, but praised by other people as pragmatic.

became the executive secretary of the National Security Council, which coordinates for the president all foreign, domestic, and military policies pertaining to the nation's security. Kissinger was one of the few people in the Nixon administration who had access to the president at almost any time of the day or night.

Both Nixon and Kissinger firmly agreed that foreign policy, given the urgent exigencies of the nuclear age, must be centralized in the Oval Office of the White House, and above all, that nothing must be done to undermine the credibility and authority of the president. Kissinger would apply these principles most rigorously throughout his eight years of service to Presidents Nixon and Ford, rarely criticizing his chief, even in private.

What developed between Nixon and Kissinger was a relationship based on professionalism. Kissinger, always deferential, never called Nixon by his first name, while, conversely, President Nixon treated Kissinger less as a subordinate than as an associate. In both private and public discussions with world leaders, Kissinger was given free rein.

Perhaps what united these two so very different men was the conviction that the highest foreign policy decision apparatus must be removed from the heavily bureaucratic State Department. ("On the whole," observed Kissinger, "if we could get rid of the bottom half of the Foreign Service we might be better off.") To achieve this goal, Nixon appointed William Rogers as his secretary of state. Rogers, whom Nixon had known from the Eisenhower years, had virtually no foreign policy experience but Nixon believed he would be absolutely trustworthy in carrying out the president's orders. "I was prepared to play a subordinate role," recalled Rogers, who admitted he knew little about foreign policy.

On actual policy, both President Nixon and Kissinger agreed that the costs of the arms race, the growing disenchantment with overseas involvements, especially Vietnam, and the emergence of new power centers around the world had made the post-World War II rivalries between the United States, the Soviet Union, and China virtually obsolete. Both men thought alike on American global strategy. Perceiving the world in traditional balance-of-power terms, Nixon was totally unwilling to cede United States influence in any part of the world where it existed. Kissinger, likewise, had reached the conclusion that President Kennedy's grand concept of America as the defender of freedom anywhere in the world was at best romantic and at worst unsupportable, given the devastating history of the

Even if they don't think Nixon is an intellect, they must realize that he has enough brains to recognize an intellect.
—White House staff member after the selection of Kissinger as assistant for national security

Nixon with Rockefeller and Kissinger in May 1969. Kissinger's misgivings about leaving the Rockefeller camp and working for Nixon—who was widely seen as a "cold warrior" and a "consummate politician" — were tempered by the opportunity to wield great power over U.S. foreign policy.

Vietnam War. In fact, Kissinger's liberal colleagues were shocked to discover that his foreign policy positions were more hardline Nixon than they had expected. Even Nixon admiringly noted, "Henry plays the game hard."

World peace was Richard Nixon's goal. This, he thought, would be his legacy to history. "After a period of confrontation," he declared in his inaugural address on January 20, 1969, "we are entering into a period of negotiation."

Like President Woodrow Wilson (1913–21), Nixon took charge of foreign policy. "All you want is a competent cabinet to run the country at home," Nixon said, "You need a president for foreign policy; no secretary of state is really important. The president makes foreign policy." And as Woodrow Wilson had used Colonel Edward M. House as his personal adviser in foreign affairs, so Nixon relied on Henry Kissinger.

Nixon with Kissinger and Secretary of State William P. Rogers aboard Air Force One in July 1971. Rogers's lack of foreign affairs experience meant that Kissinger was able to become the most powerful national security adviser in U.S. history.

47

Nixon and Kissinger in Austria, May 1972. The main issues facing the United States during the president's first term were the Vietnam War, the arms race, and relations with the Soviet Union and China. The two men sought to stress negotiation, not confrontation, as a way of attaining world peace.

Kissinger and his small staff overshadowed not only Secretary of State Rogers and the some 11,000 State Department employees, but the Department of Defense as well. Kissinger's job was to present to the president clear "options" or choices of policy, and to detail their possible consequences. In doing this, Kissinger wielded more power than any other presidential adviser in the history of the nation.

Both Nixon and Kissinger agreed that secret diplomacy, without the glare of press scrutiny, was the best way to deal with pressing foreign problems. Together, these two men developed a unique style characterized by surprise and secrecy.

The pragmatic foreign policy constructed by Nixon and Kissinger assumed that the communist world was no longer unified. Their common goal in global strategy was to maintain the current stability and order, an approach similar to the foreign policies of European nations after the Napoleonic wars (the subject of Kissinger's doctoral dissertation). Together, during Richard Nixon's first term, they collaborated on what seemed to be a remarkable series of diplomatic triumphs.

Nixon made numerous trips to foreign countries. Within a month of his inauguration, for example, he left for an eight-day working visit to Europe in order to meet other heads of state. In the summer of 1969 he traveled around the world, visiting six Asian nations as well as communist Romania, the first time an American president had visited a Soviet bloc nation. In Romania, Nixon declared, "We seek normal relations with all countries, regardless of their domestic policies."

Ironically, in May 1972, Nixon, who had made his mark on American politics for nearly 30 years as a staunch opponent of communism, became the first American president to visit the Soviet Union. At this historic summit, the leaders of the United States and the Soviet Union signed the first SALT (Strategic Arms Limitation Treaty) agreement, slowing the arms race. In these foreign policy decisions and in hundreds of others that involved American interests throughout the world, the president sought and valued Henry Kissinger's advice.

> *In the nuclear age it is no longer possible to assume that by patient accumulation of marginal advantage one can ultimately destroy one's opponent. All foreign policy has to start with that insight.*
> —HENRY KISSINGER

4

The Agony of Vietnam

Vietnam. "I cannot write about Vietnam except with pain and sadness," stated Kissinger in 1979. Indeed, pain and sadness aptly describe America's involvement in what had become a dreadful quagmire both in lives lost and in hopes for an end to what seemed an endless conflict.

Except for the Civil War, no conflict had so divided Americans as the war in Vietnam. With each passing day, it seemed that America became more and more engulfed in the complex turmoil of Southeast Asia. Growing casualty lists, secret policies, and even deceit by the executive branch under President Lyndon Baines Johnson (1963–69) contributed to domestic confusion.

Unlike World War II (1939–45), when the bombing of Pearl Harbor on December 7, 1941, marked a clear beginning of the United States's involvement, the Vietnam War had no specific starting date. Indochina had been settled by French colonists in the mid-19th century. It consisted of three old kingdoms — Laos, Cambodia, and Vietnam. During World War II, the Japanese occupied French Indochina, and the partisan underground, the na-

AP/WIDE WORLD

Ho Chi Minh, the Vietnamese Communist leader, in 1954. Ho, who studied in Paris but was trained as a communist in Moscow, led the long battle against French colonialism in Indochina and against U.S. military intervention in the region.

American soldiers carry a dead comrade out of a Vietnamese jungle in 1967. By the end of that year, nearly half a million U.S. troops were in Vietnam and the death toll had exceeded 10,000. Nonetheless, the fighting was deadlocked.

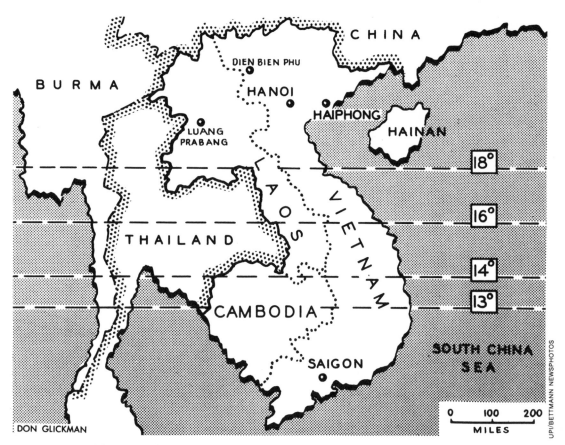

Map of Indochina. At a conference in Geneva following France's loss at Dien Bien Phu, representatives of nine powers — the United States, Great Britain, France, China, the Soviet Union, Cambodia, Laos, and the two Vietnams — agreed to divide the country along the 17th parallel while searching for an overall settlement.

tive opposition to Japanese rule, was led by a highly-skilled communist, Russian-trained Ho Chi Minh. Ho had worked against French rule long before World War II.

In September 1945, with the surrender of the Japanese, Ho Chi Minh proclaimed the independence of the Democratic Republic of Vietnam with Hanoi as its capital. The French, however, sought to maintain complete control over Indochina; they established native puppet governments in Cambodia and Laos and tried to do the same with Emperor Bao Dai in Vietnam.

In October 1949 the communists emerged victorious in China, proclaiming the People's Republic. Early in 1950 communist China recognized Ho's Hanoi government and began to give it both military and economic aid. Concerned about an emerging communist threat, many nations of Europe — Belgium, Denmark, France, Great Britain, Italy, Luxembourg, the Netherlands, Norway, and Portugal — the United States, and Canada formed the North Atlantic Treaty Organization (NATO) in 1949. (Greece, Turkey, and West Germany would join later.) Since France was an important ally, the United States, under President Harry Truman (1945–53), began to offset Chinese aid to North Vietnam with American aid to South Vietnam. By the time the United States disengaged itself from the Korean War (1950–53), America was paying more than two-thirds of the cost to maintain French military forces in Vietnam. But the American aid could not prevent total French disaster.

In 1954 the main French army was trapped and eventually defeated at Dien Bien Phu. At this point, President Dwight D. Eisenhower (1953–61) refused to commit American troops to save France's colony. On February 10, 1954, Eisenhower, with a great deal of foresight, bluntly stated: "I say that I cannot conceive of a greater tragedy for America than to get heavily involved now in an all-out war in any of those regions, particularly with large units."

On July 20, 1954, with the virtual collapse of the French army in Vietnam, representatives of nine powers — the United States, Great Britain, France, the People's Republic of China, the Soviet Union, the two Vietnams, Cambodia, and Laos — met in Geneva and worked out a complicated truce agreement. Vietnam was divided along the 17th parallel, with Ho's forces to be in the north and the French-backed Bao Dai government in the south. Elections, which had been promised, were never held because Bao Dai's prime minister Ngo Dinh Diem feared, and ruthlessly suppressed, any opposition to his growing military dictatorship in the south. Pro-communist forces in the south (Viet Cong) increasingly attacked Diem's troops. Gradually, the United States replaced France as the chief supporter of the South Vietnamese government.

Under President John F. Kennedy (1960–63), the situation in Southeast Asia continued to worsen. In May 1962 communists controlled about two-

> *There cannot be a crisis next week. My schedule is already full.*
> —HENRY KISSINGER
> as quoted in
> *The New York Times Magazine,*
> June 1, 1969

The signing of the truce between France and the North Vietnamese regime in July 1954. Despite the agreement, the situation in Southeast Asia continued to deteriorate.

thirds of Laos. By the end of 1962, acting on the advice of America's top military leaders, President Kennedy sent military instructors, pilots, and economic planners to South Vietnam. American aid increased dramatically. In addition, the U.S. Central Intelligence Agency (CIA) covertly managed to get supplies to anti-communist forces in Laos. The CIA may have also contributed to the 1963 overthrow of the Diem regime in South Vietnam, creating further political instability as nine different governments came to power between 1963 and 1968. As U.S. military commitments to South Vietnam increased, the American public generally remained uninformed of the long-range implications of this policy. Some historians claim that President Kennedy planned to withdraw all American personnel from South Vietnam by the end of 1965. He was assassinated, however, on November 22, 1963.

Under President Johnson the war dramatically escalated. On August 2 and 4, 1964, North Vietnamese torpedo boats allegedly fired on two American destroyers in the Gulf of Tonkin off the coast of North Vietnam. Johnson asked Congress to permit him to respond militarily to these unprovoked attacks. On August 7 the House of Representatives and the Senate gave the president the power he requested. Johnson regarded the congressional resolution as a virtual blank check to support his Vietnam policies.

Before the Gulf of Tonkin incident, the fighting in South Vietnam had been carried on between South Vietnamese government troops and the Viet Cong. After this incident, North Vietnam began sending its troops to fight in the south. The United States responded by actively getting involved in the war.

In February 1965, after the Viet Cong attacked an American base, Johnson ordered American planes to bomb North Vietnam. In April of that year, the president made the fateful decision that American ground troops should engage in combat. Once the war had escalated, there seemed no way to get out without damaging America's international prestige. Ho Chi Minh believed that, despite the massive American bombings, his forces would eventually outlast the United States in the war.

In fact, the war did go badly for the Americans. The Viet Cong, with their strong support from the North, matched the huge military concentration of American troops and weapons. At home, the war became the most divisive issue in decades. It led to a powerful peace movement that first centered on college campuses and then spread throughout the nation with astonishing strength. What had started as a civil war had become a major conflict between the United States and communist forces.

When Richard Nixon became president in 1969,

> *The typical political leader of the contemporary managerial society is a man of strong will, a high capacity to get himself elected, but not a very great conception of what he is going to do when he gets into office.*
> —HENRY KISSINGER
> as quoted in *Newsweek*,
> July 28, 1969

more than 500,000 Americans were fighting in Vietnam. The death toll had already reached 31,000 and the war was costing America more than $25 billion a year. More bomb tonnage was dropped on Vietnam than had been used by the Allies on all of Europe during World War II. But not a single substantive negotiating session had occurred. Protests and anguish tore America apart.

Nixon inherited this tragic situation when he took office, and from the start was determined to end American involvement. But there was no walking away from a war that had spanned four previous presidential terms, involved the country's major allies, and taken 31,000 American lives. Public opinion polls clearly showed that Americans wanted Nixon to end the war, but not by humiliating the United States. What could the president do? Should American participation in the war continue even as opposition in the United States grew? Or should Nixon admit defeat and pull out American troops? If Nixon decided to withdraw troops, would the Soviet Union be tempted to test America's strength in other parts of the world?

During the first six months of 1969, President Nixon and Henry Kissinger were moderately optimistic about negotiating a speedy end to the war. Kissinger had a plan. "Nothing to worry about," he told his former Harvard colleagues, "we'll be out in a matter of months." "Give us six months," he said to a visiting group of Quaker antiwar activists, "and if we haven't ended the war by then, you can come back and tear down the White House fence."

Kissinger encouraged Nixon to lose no time in making his intentions known to North Vietnam. On December 20, 1969, one month prior to Nixon's inauguration, Kissinger used a French friend to convey to the North Vietnam government the new administration's readiness for serious negotiations "based on the self-respect and sense of honor of all parties. The Nixon administration is prepared for an honorable settlement but for nothing less."

Kissinger proposed new negotiating procedures. One would be between Hanoi and Washington focusing exclusively on a military settlement. The sec-

ond, between Saigon and the Viet Cong, would concentrate on a political solution for South Vietnam. When both settlements were reached, an international conference would work out guarantees and safeguards for the agreements, including international peacekeeping machinery. Although Kissinger believed that the massive American troop escalation under President Johnson had been a "tragic blunder," he resisted all suggestions that the United States simply withdraw from Vietnam. Great

U.S. Secretary of Defense Robert McNamara here announces reprisal raids against North Vietnam after American naval destroyers were allegedly fired on in the Gulf of Tonkin in early August 1964. It was the first U.S. bombing mission directed at North Vietnamese territory.

U.S. F-4C Phantom jets bomb North Vietnamese targets in January 1966. Despite the massive American bombings, Ho Chi Minh believed that his forces, being more ideologically motivated, could outlast the technically superior U.S. military machine.

General William C. Westmoreland with weapons captured from the North Vietnamese, 1967. Eight months after the Gulf of Tonkin incident, American ground troops entered the war, as U.S. involvement was growing.

Anti-war demonstration in Oakland, California, 1965. As the Vietnam War spread, the American military presence there became the most divisive issue the country had faced in decades. An increasingly vocal opposition was heard on college campuses and in the streets.

nations, he reasoned, must maintain the credibility of even a mistaken commitment. "However we got into Vietnam, whatever the judgment of our actions, ending the war honorably is essential for the peace of the world. Any other solution may unloose forces that would complicate prospects for international order." For Kissinger, America's word and honor were at stake. His plan stood in marked contrast to the Pentagon's vision of a complete military victory. To the American public it seemed to be promising and to offer hope.

The North Vietnamese response demanded the withdrawal of all American forces and the replacement of the South Vietnamese Saigon government. As Kissinger wrote, "Thus was the Nixon Administration first exposed to the maddening diplomatic style of the North Vietnamese. It would have been impossible to find two societies less intended by fate to understand each other than the Vietnamese and the American. On the one side, Vietnamese history and Communist ideology combined to produce almost morbid suspicion and ferocious self-righteousness. . . . Each North Vietnamese proposal was put forward as the sole logical truth and each demand was stated in the imperative (the United States 'must'). By 1971 we had been so conditioned that when the North Vietnamese substituted 'should' for 'must' we thought great progress had been made. On the other side, there was the American belief in the efficacy of goodwill and the importance of compromise — qualities likely to be despised by dedicated Leninists who saw themselves as the inexorable spokesmen of an inevitable future, absolute truth, and superior moral insight." The North Vietnamese considered themselves in a life and death struggle. Any form of negotiations had to be seen in terms of that struggle. Gradually, the Nixon-Kissinger timetable, at first measured in months, became a thing of the past.

In March 1969 President Nixon ordered the bombing of communist positions inside Cambodia. This was hidden from the American people. Kissinger, one of the few privy to the decision, believed that this action would prevent more than 50,000 North Vietnamese troops, shuttling back and forth across Cambodian borders, from inflicting casualties on American forces and would also force the North to be more flexible in their negotiations. In April 1970 the president initiated a joint American and South Vietnamese invasion of Cambodia to attack North Vietnamese "sanctuaries" in that country.

At the same time, Nixon began withdrawing American troops from Vietnam. From a peak of 536,000 American soldiers in Vietnam in 1968, he reduced the number to 24,000 by the end of 1972. Under this policy of "Vietnamization," America armed and trained South Vietnamese troops to replace American forces. And, above all, negotiations would continue.

After the first announcement of withdrawal of

> *To win in Vietnam, we will have to exterminate a nation.*
> —DR. BENJAMIN SPOCK
> child psychologist and leading member of the anti-war movement

French soldiers in Vietnam, March 1954. Following the French defeat at Dien Bien Phu in May, and the subsequent ascendancy of the communist forces in North Vietnam, the United States became more involved in the conflict as a supporter of the South Vietnamese government.

some 25,000 American troops in June 1969, Kissinger commented, "We are now at the stage where serious negotiations should start." Kissinger sincerely wanted to believe in the negotiating process and he thought this initiative could persuade Hanoi to engage in meaningful talks to end the war. "Vietnamization," believed Kissinger, "was likely to become irreversible. Henceforth, we would be in a race between the decline in our combat capabilities and the improvement of the South Vietnamese forces — a race whose outcome was at best uncertain."

Under Nixon, the United States was on a road out of Vietnam by attempting to pursue a middle course between capitulation and the seemingly endless stalemate inherited from the Johnson administration. The American people were tired of the war, but they were not ready to be defeated. As Kissinger explained, "We considered it our painful responsibility to continue the struggle against an implacable

U.S. President Lyndon B. Johnson, troubled by the costly Vietnam War — which had taken a turn for the worse in January 1968 — stunned the nation on March 31 by announcing that he would not run for reelection.

opponent until we had achieved a fair settlement compatible with our values, our international responsibilities, and the convictions of the majority of the American people." With the withdrawal program, Nixon and Kissinger had announced their decision, which they had agreed upon even before the inauguration.

Throughout 1970 and 1971 the war widened by engulfing Laos and Cambodia. As President Nixon attempted to wind it down, the North Vietnamese escalated their offensives. In America, the outcry against the war increased. The talks continued, but "no progress" became the redundant American communication.

Kissinger, perhaps because of his ties to the

A bloodied anti-war demonstrator is arrested by a Chicago policeman during one of the violent street protests that marked the Democratic party convention in 1968. Following heated intra-party debate, Hubert H. Humphrey was chosen as the Democratic nominee for president.

EASTFOTO

A Viet Cong soldier in combat in 1971. Nixon and Kissinger wanted to end the war "honorably" so as not to diminish America's global prestige. This goal entailed the "Vietnamization" of the war — relying increasingly on South Vietnamese troops to do the fighting while American troops were withdrawn in stages.

academic community, was more sensitive to the antiwar sentiment sweeping across the college campuses than were other Nixon intimates. He felt personally bruised as antiwar protestors attacked him by name. On a visit back to Harvard for advice from his former colleagues, he found himself insulted, mistrusted, and, he thought, misunderstood. They shouted a reminder that his six months were up. He believed that if he could somehow establish a trust between American and North Vietnamese negotiators through his personal intervention, he could regain the trust that he was losing among his academic colleagues, and at the same time break the Paris peace talk deadlock and end the war.

Kissinger attended several meetings in Paris with North Vietnamese emissaries between February and

UPI/BETTMANN NEWSPHOTOS

Viet Cong prisoners being led by their American captors. As North Vietnamese forces used bases in Cambodia and Laos, the war engulfed those two countries as well.

The conventional army loses if it does not win. The guerilla army [the North Vietnamese] wins if it does not lose.

—HENRY KISSINGER

April 1970. During these talks, Kissinger's diplomatic skills were at their best. Le Duc Tho, the fifth highest member of the North Vietnamese hierarchy, represented that country. Kissinger noted that the Vietnamese leader "served his cause with dedication and skill. It was our misfortune that his cause should be to break the will of the United States and to establish Hanoi's rule over a country that we sought to defend."

These meetings, held in utmost secrecy, finally collapsed because there seemed no basis for a meaningful dialogue — "maddeningly ambiguous," in Kissinger's words. Le Duc Tho, sensing the growing American opposition to the war and the impending failure of the "Vietnamization" program, could see no reason to modify his demands for unconditional withdrawal of American forces and the overthrow of the Saigon government.

Kissinger had given negotiations a good try, but by April 1970 there was not one flicker of hope for a negotiated settlement. Kissinger thought it pointless to continue and the president agreed. Hanoi's position was unyielding — and would remain so for the next two years.

Mother and children swimming to safety during 1965. Though villages were razed and uprooted families devastated by the American assault on Vietnam, the steadfast North Vietnamese officials refused to compromise, insisting on an unconditional U.S. withdrawal.

5

The Doctrine of Force

On March 18, 1970, a surprise coup by rightist military officers in Cambodia overthrew Prince Sihanouk, the head of state. General Lon Nol, a strong anti-communist, came to power. President Nixon, in his memoirs, claims that the CIA was not involved, but Lon Nol seized power knowing that his regime would be recognized and supported by the United States.

What the prince had tried to avoid — having his kingdom directly involved in the Vietnam War — became a reality. The general immediately changed Cambodia's policy of neutrality to one of anti-communism and he asked for American military aid. This tiny country now found itself trapped in the Vietnam conflict.

Within a month thousands of communist troops had closed a ring around the capital city as Lon Nol's weak and poorly equipped army collapsed. This sudden upheaval was seen by American military officers as the opportunity to clean out communist hideaway sanctuaries that the 1969 secret bombings had missed. From these safe places in Cambodia, the communists had been crossing the border to make raids on American and South Vietnamese

Kissinger in 1972. The overthrow of Cambodia's Prince Norodom Sihanouk in March 1970 led to the U.S. invasion of that country in an attempt to root out North Vietnamese forces. Justified by Kissinger, who called it an "incursion," the move brought further turmoil to both Cambodia and the United States.

Lon Nol, the general who overthrew Prince Sihanouk. Though a skillful commander, Lon Nol was unable to pose much of a challenge to the North Vietnamese troops in Cambodia. His subsequent appeal for U.S. aid tilted Cambodia away from its position of neutrality, setting the stage for the country's deepening crisis.

UPI/BETTMANN NEWSPHOTOS

forces, then returning back to safety. Frustrated American commanders begged for a chance to strike back, but Washington insisted on respecting Cambodia's neutrality.

For Nixon, Cambodia became a challenge. It was clear from Kissinger's latest talks in Paris that the North Vietnamese were not interested in a negotiated peace. Would all of Indochina now fall to the communists? Would the "Vietnamization" program be jeopardized? And the most immediate concern, would expanded communist sanctuaries in Cambodia cause increased American casualties? Kissinger's staff began to study various plans of action for the president's consideration and, at emergency meetings of the National Security Council, Kissinger meticulously presented the options available to the president.

On April 28 President Nixon decided to use American troops to wipe out communist strongholds in Cambodia. Only a week before, he had told the American people of his plans to withdraw 150,000 troops from Vietnam. With confidence, he had declared that his policies were achieving their goals in Vietnam — and now Cambodia. Nixon knew the move into Cambodia would provoke nationwide protest, "But it is the right thing to do," concluded Nixon, "It is necessary." At no time did Kissinger express opposition to the president's decision.

Within hours of the president's announcement, violence erupted on many college campuses. The National Student Association called for Nixon's impeachment. On May 4, 1970, at Kent State University in Ohio, a group of national guardsmen, surrounded by student protestors, opened fire on them at point blank range. The guardsmen killed four of the students and wounded 11 others. That night Kissinger, deeply saddened by the Kent State tragedy, told a friend, "I'm dead. Every war has its casualties. I am a casualty of this one." After Kent State, campus disorders soared to a new hysterical pitch. On May 8 thousands of antiwar demonstrators surrounded the White House and denounced the president.

That evening, Nixon told reporters that he and

the demonstrators wanted the same things — to bring peace with honor, to end the draft, and to bring America's fighting men home from Vietnam. "I did not send these men to Vietnam," he said. The president claimed the attack on Cambodia had already succeeded in the capture of thousands of rockets and millions of rounds of small arms ammunition, thus saving hundreds, if not thousands, of American lives. All Americans, he promised, would be out of Cambodia by the end of June.

The frustration of futile negotiations, the escalation of the war, and the violence at Kent State took a heavy toll on Kissinger's morale. Not only did members of his staff resign, but former colleagues whom Kissinger had considered his most loyal friends wrote him bitter letters criticizing the administration's policies, and calling for his resignation. At one point Kissinger told Nixon, "I still think you made the right decision as far as foreign policy considerations were involved. But in view of what has

U.S. tank crew with weapons captured from communists in Cambodia, May 1970. Kissinger backed Nixon's decision to invade Cambodia, in spite of several National Security Council staff resignations over the issue.

On May 4, 1970, U.S. National Guardsmen at Ohio's Kent State University fired on students protesting the U.S. invasion of Cambodia, killing four and wounding eleven. The event sparked even more turbulent antiwar demonstrations around the country.

happened I fear I may have failed to advise you adequately of the domestic dangers." Nixon responded that he had been fully aware of both the military and political risks. "I had made the decision myself, and I assume full responsibility for it." And, concluded the president, "Henry, remember Lot's wife. Never turn back. Don't waste time rehashing things we can't do anything about."

In December 1968 Kissinger accepted the national security post and said, "The doors of my office are open to your ideas." Thirteen of Kissinger's former Harvard colleagues offered their advice, but despite their strong denunciation of the Cambodian invasion, even their cries that Nixon had gone mad, Kissinger refused to concede anything. "The president," he said, "had not lost sight of his original objective or gone off his timetable for withdrawal."

America, Kissinger believed, was distinguished from other nations by its loyalty to commitments, its trust and generosity, its bipartisan devotion to international order, its opposition to tyranny and aggression. His Harvard colleagues, Kissinger thought, had lost their perspective in their agony over Cambodia. "These are my students," he told reporters. "These are my colleagues. . . . We recognize the anguish and concern of the people who are protesting and we hope that they will recognize at some point that no group — certainly those who are in responsibility must be included — has a monopoly of anguish on the conflict."

On June 30, exactly as Nixon had announced, the last American soldiers left Cambodia. Subsequently (September 7, 1970) Kissinger met with the North Vietnamese in Paris, the first meeting since the Cambodian invasion. Later he described the meeting for Nixon, saying, "Not only did they change their tone, but they also indicated a readiness to move on substance." But a second meeting (September 27) dashed all hopes of a breakthrough. The North Vietnamese once again insisted that Washington guarantee their political victory in the South before they would allow the United States to withdraw "with honor." Kissinger broke off the meeting without setting a date for another, and the diplomatic stalemate once again led to additional military action.

On February 8, 1971, South Vietnamese forces supported by American air power moved against the "Ho Chi Minh trails" in Laos — trails which served as conduits to move military supplies from North Vietnam through Laos to South Vietnam. Kissinger had little enthusiasm for this operation, but did nothing to stop it: "The operation, conceived in doubt and assailed by skepticism, proceeded in con-

Emotions are of no use. Least of all are they of any use in helping one to attain peace.
—HENRY KISSINGER
speaking in 1972
concerning the
Paris peace talks

American soldiers and helicopters in Vietnam, 1971. With the Paris negotiations between Kissinger and Le Duc Tho showing little progress, President Nixon decided to mine and bomb Haiphong harbor in an attempt to force a cease-fire. Some commentators called the tactic "jugular" diplomacy.

Peace demonstration in Washington, D.C., May 1972.
Though by this time most of the American troops had
been withdrawn from Vietnam, the fighting remained
fierce and domestic opposition to U.S. policy persisted.

Wounded American military advisers being rescued in April 1972. Nixon's action in Haiphong — about which Kissinger was said to have doubts — was prompted by a massive invasion of South Vietnam by communist forces, which threatened the administration's Vietnamization strategy.

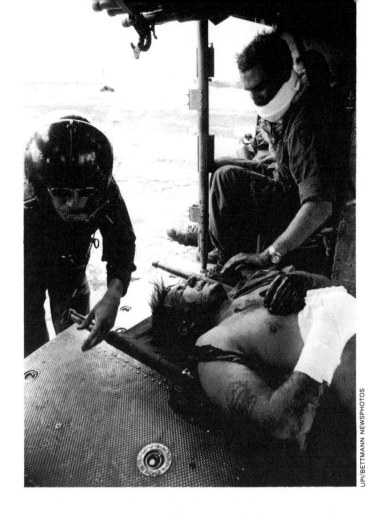

UPI/BETTMANN NEWSPHOTOS

We are the unwilling, led by the unqualified, doing the unnecessary, for the ungrateful.
    —graffiti on G.I. helmets during the Vietnam War

fusion." He perceived every military action as a prelude to negotiation. The South Vietnamese army was pulled out 44 days after the maneuver began, but only after thousands of South Vietnamese lives were lost. American correspondents described it as a rout.

"There was no goal to which I was more passionately committed than to restore the unity and cohesion of my adopted country by ending its agony in Vietnam through negotiation," wrote Kissinger. "Nixon," he observed, "was always more skeptical than I that any negotiations would succeed until there had been a military showdown. He turned out to be right."

Kissinger returned to the Paris negotiation table in late May 1971 with a new plan. The United States, for the first time, gave up its demand for mutual troop withdrawal, agreeing to withdraw most of its forces unilaterally, provided Hanoi agreed to end all additional infiltration into Indochina. The political future of South Vietnam was to be left to the South Vietnamese to settle and Kissinger repeated the demand for the immediate release by both sides of all prisoners of war.

The meetings lasted three months, but Hanoi remained unwilling to enter a cease-fire agreement or to return prisoners unless the United States first

Young victims of American napalm bombs, June 1972.

agreed to assist in establishing a communist-controlled government in Saigon. The prize of peace remained as far away as ever.

On March 30, 1972, the North Vietnamese, with Soviet-made equipment, including tanks and long-range artillery, invaded the South with an estimated 120,000 troops. The intensity of the invasion shocked Kissinger. Nixon, who had warned for years that he would react strongly to such a North Vietnamese offensive, quickly responded with massive aerial attacks on the North, as well as with an air and sea blockade.

This action re-ignited the antiwar movement in the United States, but Nixon believed, as did Kissinger, that peace could only be achieved through sustained military action. The press hinted that Nixon would even order the dikes of North Vietnam destroyed, causing untold civilian casualties.

At this point, it seemed that Kissinger was directing the military — leaning over large maps, telling admirals to move fleets, and barking orders to generals. "If we were to run out of Vietnam under these conditions," stated Kissinger, "our entire foreign policy would be in jeopardy. Hanoi had committed so many resources to the effort that once stopped, it would almost certainly be obliged to settle. I asked every agency to give absolute priority to defeating the offensive."

On May 2 Kissinger went to Paris again to resume his talks with Le Duc Tho. It seemed that this time Kissinger made progress — he announced that an agreement was finally close at hand. Both Kissinger and Nixon thought the American offer could bring a quick end to the fighting: If the North Vietnamese would agree to a cease-fire and return American prisoners, that and nothing more, the United States would withdraw from Vietnam within four months. This time, Kissinger thought he and Le Duc Tho had reached an agreement. Soviet Premier Leonid Brezhnev had told Kissinger that Hanoi was likely to be flexible, and that there was reason to be optimistic. Nixon, with the American presidential election approaching, was especially eager to put the Vietnam War behind him.

Still, Le Duc Tho rejected Nixon's offer. "I'd say, 'How about de-escalation and a cease-fire?' They'd say, 'Wars aren't fought to have a cease-fire. Wars are fought to have victory.' I'd say, 'How about de-escalation alone?' They'd say, 'We don't fight to de-escalate.' " Le Duc Tho still wanted a communist government in Saigon and did not want to negotiate. A weary Kissinger returned to Washington, depressed and dejected.

Nixon quickly responded militarily — the railway from China was to be bombed, and Haiphong har-

Kissinger and National Security Council chief deputy Alexander Haig (in the center) return from the Paris negotiations in October 1972. A breakthrough had been achieved during this round of talks, leading Kissinger to declare that "peace is at hand."

American B-52 bombers. As the peace talks hit more snags, Nixon, in late 1972, ordered massive air attacks on installations in and around Hanoi and Haiphong. The so-called Christmas bombing was the most concentrated air offensive of the Vietnam War.

bor, the port for Hanoi, would be mined, thus stopping both Chinese aid and shipments from the Soviet Union. This was to be the "last resort" position. (Kissinger met with the Soviet ambassador to stress that the United States was not seeking a confrontation with the Russians.) "If anyone had predicted," Kissinger later admitted, "that by May 8, we'd wind up in this position, I wouldn't have believed it."

In August 1972 Kissinger again met with Le Duc Tho in Paris. The meeting lasted eight hours — "the most interesting session we have ever had," Kissinger told Nixon. The North Vietnamese were willing

Ruined homes and buildings in Haiphong, 1972.

to accept a coalition government in Saigon with the communists having one-third representation; non-communists, a third; and "neutralists," the final third. American policy firmly opposed any coalition government, but Kissinger believed, at last, that Hanoi was willing to make concessions. Intricate negotiations continued through August — "It required an advanced degree in metaphysics to understand the bewildering series [of proposals] he [Le Duc Tho] was now putting before us." But the United States remained adamant in its support for its Saigon ally.

After the November 1972 presidential election, certainly a stunning reelecting mandate for Nixon, the president ordered a massive attack on Hanoi and other North Vietnamese cities. The targets included docks, airfields, railyards, power plants,

Secretary of State Rogers signing the peace agreement in Paris on January 27, 1973. Despite the landmark treaty, the military and political situation in Vietnam remained highly volatile; indeed, it was not long before the North Vietnamese resumed their efforts to reunify the country.

UPI/BETTMANN NEWSPHOTOS

Kissinger and Le Duc Tho in Paris, early 1973. The Christmas bombing brought the North Vietnamese negotiator back to the bargaining table, where he and Kissinger quickly resolved their differences. President Nixon subsequently stated, "We have finally achieved peace with honor."

anti-aircraft defenses, and the like. Since these were located in or near residential areas, neither schools nor hospitals could be spared. The destruction was achieved at considerable cost to the United States. In the previous seven years of the war only one B-52 bomber had been lost. Now, in the short span of two weeks, 15 of the planes had been brought down by surface-to-air missiles. Still, Nixon achieved his end. North Vietnam had suffered such internal calamity that subsequent negotiations between Kissinger and Le Duc Tho finally produced a cease-fire agreement on January 27, 1973.

"Peace with honor," a jubilant President Nixon announced. But public reaction to the end of the longest war in American history was not one of jubilation. The joyful celebrations that followed World War I and World War II did not take place in the aftermath of the Vietnam War. What remained instead were questions regarding the enormous price both sides paid in waging the war and how long the fragile peace could last. It was for these tortuous, tedious negotiations, which spanned four years — and the final result, a cease-fire in Vietnam — that both Le Duc Tho and Henry Kissinger shared the 1973 Nobel Peace Prize.

The superpowers often behave like two heavily armed blind men feeling their way around a room, each believing himself in moral peril from the other whom he assumes to have perfect vision.
—HENRY KISSINGER

6

Rapprochement with China

> *History knows no resting places and no plateaus.*
> —HENRY KISSINGER
> in his book
> *The White House Years,*
> published in 1979

On July 15, 1971, President Nixon announced in a radio broadcast that he was going to visit China the following year "to seek the normalization of relations between the two countries." Behind this announcement, which instantly dominated the headlines of the world's newspapers, lay more than 30 months of complex diplomatic signals and negotiations directed by Henry Kissinger.

Since the communists had gained control of China in 1949, the United States had prohibited trade with the mainland, refused to recognize the government of Mao Zedong, and opposed that country's membership in the United Nations. For 20 years there had been virtual diplomatic isolation and ideological hostility between the two countries. During the Korean War, American and Chinese soldiers had fought against each other; and many American policy-makers considered the Vietnam War part of Chinese expansion.

Washington continued to recognize Chiang Kaishek's Nationalist government on the island of Taiwan as the official government of China. From 1949

Chinese soldiers patrol Chenpao island on the Sino-Soviet border. In the late 1960s, steadily mounting tensions with the Soviet Union made China more receptive to normalizing relations with the United States.

President Nixon and Chinese Premier Zhou Enlai during Nixon's visit to Beijing in February 1972. The normalization of relations between the two superpowers was set in motion by Kissinger's secret contacts with Chinese officials over the course of 30 months.

AP/WIDE WORLD

until Nixon's dramatic radio broadcast, no American in national politics had opposed the recognition of the Beijing government more resolutely than had Richard Nixon. Now making a complete turnabout, he reopened relations with a spectacular display of presidential diplomacy.

"We took even ourselves by surprise," wrote Kissinger. "Originally we had not thought reconciliation possible. We were convinced that the Chinese were fanatic and hostile. But even though we could not initially see a way to achieve it, both Nixon and I believed in the importance of an opening to the People's Republic of China."

The time was right for such an effort since Chinese leaders also reached the conclusion that a fundamental shift in policy towards the United States was necessary. Tensions had been mounting between the Soviet Union and China, and there had even been recent armed clashes along their common borders. Kissinger had taken precautions, preparing contingency plans for American policy in case of a Sino-Soviet war, as such an event would upset the global balance of power.

Once Nixon reached the conclusion that the United States "should give every encouragement . . . to exploring possibilities of rapprochement with the Chinese," he left it to Kissinger to implement the strategy and the diplomacy. Soon thereafter it was agreed that Henry Kissinger would meet secretly with Chinese officials in order to arrange a Nixon visit to the People's Republic. When Nixon realized that the first step had become reality, he buoyantly took Kissinger to the Lincoln Sitting Room, a Victorian parlor in the southeast corner of the White House, found some brandy and two glasses, and proposed a toast to what had been and what remained to be done.

For the next months, Nixon raised questions and Kissinger would try to answer them. Together, they reviewed the issues that would come up during Kissinger's secret visit. Together they wrote the opening statement Kissinger would read to Chinese Premier Zhou Enlai and a dozen or so hypothetical Chinese communiqués that Kissinger, on behalf of

Kissinger with Zhou Enlai, October 1971. The two dynamic statesmen were impressed with each other and established a personal rapport. Kissinger was said to have been particularly taken with Zhou's comment, "There is turmoil under the heavens, and we have the opportunity to end this."

the president, could accept.

The first Kissinger-Enlai exchange in Beijing, which took place on July 9, 1971, set the tone. "Just damned exciting," one White House aide later remarked after reading Kissinger's 40 pages of firsthand impressions. Kissinger, who had been concerned that the presence of U.S. naval ships in the Taiwan Strait would strain relations, was surprised to discover that Zhou Enlai considered Vietnam a more troubling issue. Zhou impressed Kissinger with his intelligence and subtle manner. Most important, Kissinger's trip to China paved the way for dialogue and cordial relations between China and the United States.

Kissinger now began planning the president's trip. "What we are attempting to do with the People's

Republic," he told reporters, "is not to have a visit. What we are attempting to do is start an historic evolution."

Nixon arrived in China on February 21, 1972. "I know of no presidential trip that was so carefully planned, nor of any president who ever prepared himself so conscientiously," wrote Kissinger of the American leader's visit. "Nixon read all the briefing books with exquisite care."

For one week, American television, with Chinese cooperation, followed the president and his entourage. Nixon was shown visiting the Great Wall and the famous tombs of the Ming emperors, dining with Chinese leaders at sumptuous feasts, and exchanging pleasantries with Communist party leader Mao Zedong and Premier Zhou. Meanwhile, behind

From left: Zhou Enlai, interpreter Tang Wen Sheng, Chinese Communist party leader Mao Zedong, Nixon, and Kissinger during the 1972 visit. The historic trip to China was perhaps Nixon's greatest diplomatic triumph.

AP/WIDE WORLD

President and Mrs. Nixon visit the Great Wall of China in February 1972.

91

UPI/BETTMANN NEWSPHOTOS

Nixon and Zhou toast each other at a banquet held in the president's honor in Beijing's Great Hall of the People on February 21, 1972. Despite differences over the status of Taiwan, the Vietnam War, and other issues, the two leaders pledged that they would work toward peaceful coexistence.

closed doors, the president and his aides talked with their Chinese counterparts about more normal relations. Never before had any summit meeting been so carefully prepared and so elaborately staged. One effect was to reduce the anti-Chinese feeling many Americans had held for more than a generation.

The summit was a stunning diplomatic success. In addition to agreeing to scientific, cultural, and other exchanges, one year after Nixon's visit the two nations set up "liaison offices," essentially embassies, in each other's capitals.

By 1973 it seemed that relations with China were improving after nearly a quarter century of estrangement. Although major problems between the two nations remained unsolved, especially the war in Vietnam, the reopening of the door to China was a great diplomatic victory for President Nixon and for his foreign policy adviser Henry Kissinger. During a banquet in Beijing, Zhou Enlai and Kissinger toasted one another, clinking glasses of *mao tai*, a strong Chinese liquor. They knew they had done their work well.

Kissinger and Zhou, November 1973. In the year after Nixon's historic visit, valuable scientific and cultural exchange programs between China and the United States were established.

7

Secretary of State

Kissinger's four years as President Nixon's national security adviser had brought him recognition as one of the world's finest diplomats. He had been the most influential of the president's advisers, and had also proven himself to be the most polished and persuasive of Nixon's public spokesmen. Republicans and Democrats alike applauded his diplomatic skill and his vast knowledge of history and world affairs. But Kissinger thought it time for him to leave the administration — so much of what he and Nixon started out to accomplish in 1969 had been done. With the end of American involvement in the Vietnam War, Kissinger believed the nation to be on the threshold of one of the great creative periods in United States foreign policy. "Oh, you can't say permanent peace," he conceded, "but at least you can help set the structure in place."

In four years Kissinger had risen from adviser to celebrity to superstar. Following his divorce, Kissinger had stepped into the international social spotlight. He was frequently seen in the company of movie starlets and other glamorous jetsetters, earning a reputation as a swinger. Both professionally

UPI/BETTMANN NEWSPHOTOS

Former White House counsel John W. Dean III testifies before the Senate Watergate Committee on June 23, 1973. Dean's revelations linked the White House to various illegal schemes and began the process that led, ultimately, to President Nixon's resignation in 1974.

Nixon and Kissinger on September 22, 1973, after Kissinger was sworn in as America's secretary of state. As Nixon became embroiled in the Watergate scandal, the appointment of Kissinger, a strong steward of foreign affairs, was considered an absolute necessity.

and socially, Kissinger was soaring. In December 1972 *Time* magazine selected Nixon and Kissinger joint "Men of the Year" and the Gallup Poll (a national survey) listed Kissinger, now somewhat of a culture hero, as the fourth most admired man in America.

It is frequently claimed that to be a successful presidential adviser one must remain in the shadows, out of the spotlight. For Kissinger this was no longer possible. "The intangible bond between president and assistant," he observed, "had become too frayed for me to be able to function much longer." As a result of his major diplomatic successes — China, Vietnam, the strengthening of the Atlantic Alliance, the SALT agreement — Kissinger had become too visible. He told his closest associates that he would resign towards the end of 1973, satisfied that Vietnam had been settled, and new and positive relations were developing between Washington, Moscow, and Beijing.

In August 1973 the president and his immediate staff were vacationing in San Clemente, California. One hot afternoon, Nixon's daughter, Julie, telephoned Kissinger to invite him and his family to come for a swim in the Nixon pool. "I got my swimming trunks and walked over from my office, past the helicopter pad, to the Nixon quarters," recalled Kissinger. "Soon Nixon appeared and joined me and my children in the water. After a minute he suggested we go to the shallow end of the pool and chat about his news conference scheduled for the next morning. . : . I sat on the steps of the pool; the president of the United States floated on his back in the water. Matter-of-factly we reviewed some answers he proposed to give to foreign policy questions. Suddenly, without warmth or enthusiasm, he said: 'I shall open the press conference by announcing your appointment as secretary of state.' It was the first time he had mentioned the subject to me." Kissinger replied lamely that he hoped to justify the president's confidence. "In fact," Kissinger wrote, "both Nixon and I knew there was no other choice."

A major scandal called Watergate (named after the Watergate Hotel in Washington D.C., where the

Democratic National Committee had its offices) was engulfing the president. In May, only six months after Nixon's sweeping reelection victory, a special Senate committee began to hold public hearings about illegalities committed during the 1972 presidential campaign. As millions watched on television, a parade of witnesses testified that the White House staff and the Committee to Re-Elect the President had conspired to conduct and later to cover up an illegal operation aimed at sabotaging the Democratic party's 1972 presidential campaign.

Kissinger with presidential aides H. Robert Haldeman (left) and John Ehrlichman, both of whom spent time in prison for their roles in the Watergate affair. Kissinger, immersed in foreign affairs, was shocked at Nixon's apparent involvement in what he called a "pointless" domestic exercise.

In the Nixon administration there had been an almost total separation between the domestic and the foreign policy advisers. Not only was Kissinger unaware of the White House involvement in the alleged illegalities, but he was absolutely shocked as the scandalous drama unfolded. He wrote, "I could not imagine that a president as politically experienced as Nixon would permit the White House to be involved in so pointless an exercise." Kissinger noticed that the president, who had always immersed himself in foreign policy, seemed preoccupied with domestic problems. Memoranda were returned without his usual lengthy notations, and on at least one occasion, Nixon had checked every box of an options paper, defeating its purpose.

In April 1973 Kissinger reached the conclusion that Watergate "was bound to rock the nation" and it could have "grave implications for the president." One of Nixon's closest political friends had informed Kissinger, in the utmost confidence, that "the

Kissinger, Rogers, Soviet leader Leonid Brezhnev, and Nixon at the Moscow summit in May 1972. During the trip the Strategic Arms Limitation Treaty (SALT) was signed, the first bilateral attempt to put a ceiling on the development of nuclear weapons.

administration seemed headed for prolonged turmoil without a foreseeable outcome."

Kissinger was extremely dismayed by the Watergate scandal. "For four years, I had sustained myself through the anguishing turmoil of Vietnam with the vision of a united America turning at last to tasks of construction. And now through acts that made no sense, discord would descend once again on a society already weakened by ten years of upheaval. I felt like a swimmer who had already survived dangerous currents only to be plucked from apparent safety by unexpected and even more violent riptides toward uncharted seas."

Month after month the Watergate investigation linked the highest levels of the Nixon administration to one illegal scheme after another. (Unrelated to Watergate, the vice-president of the United States, Spiro Agnew, charged with bribe-taking when governor of Maryland, resigned in October 1973.) The scandalous unfolding of events debilitated Nixon, and even threatened the very institution of the presidency. When Nixon appointed Kissinger secretary of state, he realized that it was essential to have a strong individual in the position, one who could administer U.S. foreign policy notwithstanding current domestic uncertainties.

Secretary of State Kissinger found himself dominating foreign policy as Nixon's ability to govern disintegrated. "We did not know the dimensions of the looming scandal. . . . We would try jointly to develop policies and initiatives to maintain the confidence of the American people in their government even in the midst of a political crisis."

In the midst of Watergate, the Middle East erupted in crisis. From almost the first day he became national security adviser, Kissinger had tried to arrange a peace settlement among Egypt, Syria, and Israel. In the region, the United States had backed Israel with military and economic support, while the Soviet Union had helped arm Egypt and Syria. The continued plight of Palestinian refugees and the demand for an independent Palestinian state had complicated Kissinger's efforts.

Then, on October 6, 1973, exactly two weeks after

Without question Kissinger's personal attributes, his views, and his procedures have all entered, subtly or blatantly, into the formation and execution of American foreign policy during a critical period marked especially by the problems of deterrence, détente, and America's involvement in Vietnam.
—BRUCE MAZLISH
American historian

99

Kissinger had been sworn in as secretary of state, fighting broke out as Egypt and Syria attacked Israel on the Jewish holy day of Yom Kippur. Both sides suffered heavy casualties, but Israel soon demonstrated its military superiority. At the same time, an oil embargo, imposed by Arab oil-producing nations in an effort to stop the United States from supporting Israel, raised havoc with available domestic supplies, sent gasoline prices skyrocketing, and made urgent the long-debated energy question.

The war surprised Kissinger, who had believed that the volatile Middle East was under control. With Nixon's approval, he set about negotiating a cease-fire agreement between Israel and Egypt, which was reached on October 22, 1973.

But strong, threatening charges by the Soviet Union against the United States for its assistance to Israel forced the president to place American armed forces on a worldwide alert. At a news conference, Kissinger was stunned when a reporter speculated that this alert had been prompted by the need to divert the public's attention from Watergate rather than by the real requirements of diplomacy in the Middle East. Taken aback, Kissinger replied that it was a symptom of what was happening to

Tennessee Senator Howard Baker (left) and North Carolina Senator Sam Ervin, Jr., who headed the Senate Watergate probe, during a hearing in July 1973. Kissinger, too, was touched by the scandal when it was revealed that he had advised the president regarding wiretaps of 13 government officials and 4 newsmen.

UPI/BETTMANN NEWSPHOTOS

the nation even to suggest that the United States would be thus motivated. "There has to be a minimum of confidence," he said, "that the senior officials of the American government are not playing with the lives of the American people."

On November 5, 1973, Secretary of State Kissinger (and still national security adviser, since he retained that post until 1975), took the first of his many trips to the Middle East aimed at establishing peace in the region. In an unparalleled display of diplomacy, he personally guided first Israel and Egypt, and then Israel and Syria, along the painful road toward a peaceful settlement of their differences. In fact, the Middle East occupied most of Kissinger's time into mid-1974.

Kissinger shuttled between Tel Aviv, Israel, and Damascus, Syria, in a grueling attempt to disengage their forces. The negotiations took the form of an endless series of haggles. At every critical point, the Syrians and the Israelis went to the edge of the abyss and spoke of renewed war. And then they drew back. Both sides mistrusted each other, but they could not bring themselves to give up their first real chance for peace. Using skills he honed during the Paris peace talks, Kissinger patiently assisted the Syrians and the Israelis in reaching a military disengagement, which they did on May 31, 1974.

Indeed, this first step toward peace was a major diplomatic achievement of Kissinger's career; if Syria would sign an agreement with Israel, perhaps there would be no ideological obstacles to peace talks with other Arab states. A physically exhausted and emotionally drained Kissinger had spent 34 days traveling between Damascus and Tel Aviv. His efforts paid off. He had served as a successful catalyst in bridging differences between these two adversaries. Public acclaim for the secretary of state was unprecedented. Commentators described his diplomatic skills in the most superlative terms. A *Newsweek* cover showed him in a "Superman" suit and the Gallup Poll this time reported Kissinger to be the most admired man in America.

In addition to this high public acclaim for his diplomatic successes, Kissinger was enjoying a new

Always give your best, never get discouraged, never be petty; always remember, others may hate you. Those who hate you don't win unless you hate them. And then you destroy yourself.
—RICHARD NIXON
in his final address to his cabinet before leaving office, August 9, 1974

AP/WIDE WORLD

Secretary of State Kissinger and actress Jill St. John attend a reception in 1973. Kissinger's popularity soared in the early 1970s; often photographed in the company of stars, he assumed the status of a popular celebrity himself.

UPI/BETTMANN NEWSPHOTOS

Spiro Agnew announces his resignation from the vice-presidency on October 10, 1973. Agnew was forced to leave office because of corruption that occurred while he was governor of Maryland in the mid-1960s. He subsequently was convicted on a charge of tax evasion.

development in his personal life. In March 1974 Kissinger married Nancy Sharon Maginnes, a Rockefeller associate whom Kissinger had met in 1965. The couple's Acapulco honeymoon was a major media event, and Kissinger basked in the spotlight.

But these celebrated diplomatic strides were not due solely to Kissinger's efforts. No secretary of state can make policy; only the president has such authority. Kissinger rightfully credited President Nixon's perseverance in the face of a hesitant State Department bureaucracy, America's vacillating allies, a nervous Soviet Union, and the passionate combatants in the Middle East, in the quest for the

Israeli tank. Just two weeks after being named secretary of state, Kissinger received a trial by fire when Egypt and Syria launched a war against Israel. Kissinger negotiated a cease-fire and then a peace settlement through what came to be known as "shuttle diplomacy" for his frequent trips around the region.

UNITED STATES OF AMERICA

Kissinger and other tired representatives in December 1973. The Middle East occupied most of Kissinger's time through mid-1974, and his success there made him, according to a Gallup poll taken at the time, the most admired man in America.

Syrian-Israeli disengagement agreement.

The president made a triumphant tour of Middle East capitals in June 1974. Millions of delirious Egyptians greeted him in Cairo, Alexandria, and every village in between. The king of Saudi Arabia toasted Nixon in Jidda; the president of Syria warmly welcomed him to Damascus; and he became the first president to visit Israel.

Later, in June, Nixon went to Moscow for his third summit with Soviet leaders. But nothing the president did could ease the effect that the Watergate scandal was having on his administration.

> *I've always acted alone. Americans admire the cowboy leading the caravan alone astride his horse, the cowboy entering a village or city alone on his horse. Without even a pistol, maybe, because he doesn't go in for shooting. This romantic character suits me.*
> —HENRY KISSINGER

AP/WIDE WORLD

Gas line in New York City, early 1974. In an effort to end U.S. support for Israel, Arab oil-producing nations imposed an oil embargo. The action harmed the American economy and put further pressure on Kissinger's diplomatic efforts.

In July 1974 the House of Representatives Judiciary Committee voted three articles of impeachment against the president. Surprisingly, a poll taken that same month showed that all but 13% of the public still thought that Nixon was inspiring confidence as president, and that motions to remove him from office were unjustified.

At 5:58 P.M. on the afternoon of August 7, 1974, Kissinger received an urgent call requesting that he come right over to the White House. When he arrived he found Nixon dejected, alone in the Oval Office, gazing out at the rose garden through the bay windows. Kissinger later wrote, "I knew the feeling. . . . I had left the place where I had been brought up to emigrate to a foreign land: attempting to say goodbye to something familiar and beloved, to absorb it, so to speak, so that one can never be separated from it." Nixon turned when he heard Kissinger enter the room, and proceeded to tell him of his decision to resign.

Nixon understood that the office of the presidency, and indeed his own place in history, would

Kissinger and second wife, Nancy, attend a ceremony in Wales, 1975. They had met in 1965, when Nancy was working for Rockefeller, and were married in 1974.

GOD BLESS NIXON. PEACE FOR THE LAND OF PEACE WE TRUST NI... MAN HONOUR FOR HONORAB...

Nixon and Egyptian President Anwar al Sadat parade through Alexandria in a motorcade on June 13, 1974. Kissinger's successful negotiations for a disengagement agreement between Egypt and Israel paved the way for an improvement in relations between Egypt and the United States.

Kissinger and Rockefeller, January 3, 1975. Kissinger went on to serve Nixon's successor, Gerald R. Ford, as secretary of state until the end of Ford's term in 1976. Rockefeller, meanwhile, served as Ford's vice-president.

better survive his resignation than his impeachment. He also knew that U.S. foreign policy, which Nixon and Kissinger had worked so hard to advance, would be jeopardized less by his resignation than by a constitutional crisis such as the impeachment of the president.

"History will treat you more kindly than your contemporaries have," he told the president. Kissinger recalls putting his arm around Nixon, finally bridging the personal distance that had separated them for all their working years — "and if I did not in fact embrace him, I felt as if I had."

On August 9, 1974, President Nixon formally resigned from office, the first president in American history to do so.

Nixon's farewell speech, August 9, 1974. First Lady Patricia and daughter Tricia are at right. Two days earlier, when Nixon told Kissinger of his decision to resign, Kissinger told him, "History will treat you more kindly than your contemporaries have."

Kissinger remained secretary of state under Gerald Ford, Nixon's successor. Ford also asked Nelson Rockefeller to serve as his vice-president, a move that certainly had Kissinger's support. Ford and Rockefeller thus became the first non-elected president and vice-president in the nation's history. On no foreign policy issue was there a discernible difference between Ford and Nixon. Kissinger served as secretary of state until the end of Ford's term in 1976.

The 1973 cease-fire agreement had not brought lasting peace in Vietnam. After American troops withdrew, the fighting continued with both North and South Vietnam violating the truce. America continued to back the South with economic and military aid. The war's end came unexpectedly. In March 1975 the president of South Vietnam ordered his forces to abandon several outlying provinces, and a headlong retreat quickly ensued. Within weeks, communist troops were moving in on Saigon. The South Vietnamese president fled, the army simply collapsed, and thousands tried to flee the country in a chaotic exodus. In late April, Saigon surrendered. At the same time, Cambodia fell to communist control, and Laos came under communist influence. Americans had learned a most difficult and painful lesson about the limits of power. An era in American history had ended.

Leaving office on January 20, 1977, Kissinger continued his work as a consultant, lecturer, and writer on various topics in world politics, international relations, and diplomacy. In 1982 he founded Kissinger Associates, a consulting firm assisting companies to develop overseas interests and make long-range foreign policy evaluations bearing on those interests.

Kissinger with Ronald Reagan in September 1980, before the latter's election to the presidency. Kissinger has remained an influential voice in international affairs as an occasional adviser to Reagan and as a private consultant, lecturer, and writer on world politics.

Further Reading

Ashman, Charles. *Kissinger: The Adventures of Super-Kraut.* New York: Dell Publishing Co., 1972.

Blumenfeld, Ralph, et al. *Henry Kissinger: The Private and Public Story.* New York: New American Library, 1974.

Graubard, Stephen. *Kissinger: Portrait of a Mind.* New York: W. W. Norton & Co., 1973.

Hersh, Seymour M. *The Price of Power: Kissinger in the Nixon White House.* New York: Summit Books, 1983.

Kalb, Bernard and Marvin Kalb. *Kissinger.* Boston: Little, Brown & Co., 1974.

Karnow, Stanley. *Vietnam: A History.* New York: The Viking Press, 1983.

Kissinger, Henry. *American Foreign Policy.* New York: W. W. Norton & Co., 1969.

———. *The Necessity for Choice.* New York: W. W. Norton & Co., 1961.

———. *Nuclear Weapons and Foreign Policy.* New York: W. W. Norton & Co., 1969.

———. *White House Years.* Boston: Little, Brown & Co., 1979.

———. *Years of Upheaval.* Boston: Little, Brown & Co., 1982.

Landau, David. *Kissinger: The Uses of Power.* Boston: Houghton Mifflin Co., 1972.

Mazlish, Bruce. *Kissinger: The European Mind in American Policy.* New York: Basic Book Publishers, 1976.

Nixon, Richard. *The Memoirs of Richard Nixon.* New York: Grosset & Dunlap, 1978.

Chronology

May 27, 1923	Born Heinz Alfred Kissinger in the Bavarian city of Fürth
1938	Flees Nazi Germany with family and settles in New York City
1944	Returns to Germany with U.S. Army to fight the Nazis
1945	Directs recovery efforts in two German districts
1947–50	Attends Harvard University, receiving a B.A. in government
1950–56	Does graduate work at Harvard, receiving a Ph.D.
1951	Named executive director of the Harvard International Seminar
1952	Establishes *Confluence*, a journal on international affairs
1956–57	Heads research project for the Council on Foreign Relations; writes best-selling book, *Nuclear Weapons and Foreign Policy*
1957	Hired by Harvard as assistant professor of government
1957–58	Directs a study of American foreign policy funded by the Rockefeller Brothers Fund
1961–62	Serves as consultant to President John F. Kennedy on military and security policy
Nov. 5, 1968	Richard M. Nixon is elected president of the United States and appoints Kissinger as national security adviser
June 1969	25,000 U.S. troops are withdrawn from Vietnam, beginning "Vietnamization"
Feb. 20, 1970	Kissinger begins secret peace talks in Paris with North Vietnamese delegation headed by Le Duc Tho
April–May 1970	Nixon orders invasion of Cambodia; four student protesters at Kent State killed by national guardsmen
July 1971	Kissinger makes first of two visits to the People's Republic of China to arrange for Nixon's historic trip
Feb. 21, 1972	Nixon arrives in China
April 20, 1972	Kissinger goes to Moscow to prepare Nixon's first summit meeting with Soviet leader Leonid Brezhnev in May
Nov. 7, 1972	Nixon re-elected, defeating Senator George McGovern
Jan. 27, 1973	Kissinger and Le Duc Tho sign a cease-fire agreement
May 1973	Senate subcommittee begins investigation of activities of the Committee to Re-Elect the President during the 1972 campaign
Aug. 22, 1973	Kissinger appointed secretary of state (also retains position as national security adviser until 1975)
Oct. 16, 1973	Awarded the Nobel Peace Prize
May 31, 1974	Syria and Israel sign a military disengagement engineered by Kissinger
Aug. 9, 1974	Nixon becomes the first president in American history to resign from office, and is succeeded by Gerald Ford
April 30, 1975	South Vietnamese capital of Saigon falls to the North Vietnamese
Jan. 20, 1977	Kissinger leaves office

Index

Fred L. Israel is Professor of American History at the City College of New York. His previous books include *Nevada's Key Pittmann* and *A History of American Presidential Elections*, which he co-edited with Arthur M. Schlesinger, jr. He is also the author of *Franklin Delano Roosevelt* in the Chelsea House series WORLD LEADERS   PAST & PRESENT.

Arthur M. Schlesinger, jr., taught history at Harvard for many years and is currently Albert Schweitzer Professor of the Humanities at City University of New York. He is the author of numerous highly praised works in American history and has twice been awarded the Pulitzer Prize. He served in the White House as special assistant to presidents Kennedy and Johnson.